D0518936

The Faber Book of Greek Legends

also edited by Kathleen Lines

THE FABER STORYBOOK

TALES OF MAGIC AND ENCHANTMENT

THE FABER BOOK OF
Greek Legends

edited by
KATHLEEN LINES

illustrated by Faith Jaques

FABER AND FABER
London · Boston

292·08
LW

First published in 1973
by Faber and Faber Limited
3 Queen Square London WC1
Reprinted 1975 and 1979
Printed in Great Britain by
Whitstable Litho Ltd.,
Whitstable, Kent
All rights reserved

ISBN 0 571 09830 4

This collection © Faber and Faber Ltd, 1973
Foreword and the booklist 'Other
Retellings' © Kathleen Lines, 1973

FOR DEB'S GRANDCHILDREN
WITH LOVE FROM K

Contents

CONTENTS

The Stories: Authors and Sources

Dennis Butts	'The Childhood of Achilles'*
	'The Homecoming of Agamemnon'*
	(based on the *Oresteia* of Aeschylus)
A. J. Church	'Achilles and the Death of Hector'
	extracts with some editing from *The Story of the Iliad* (Seeley and Co 1891)
	'Helen of Troy' (in part, from the same book)
Roger Lancelyn Green	'Erigone and Her Dog' (slightly altered with the author's permission) from *Tales the Muses Told* (Bodley Head 1965)
Charles Lamb	'Odysseus and Circe' (an extract from *The Adventures of Ulysses* 1808, in parts edited)
Andrew Lang	'Helle and Phrixus' ('The Children of the Cloud', lightly edited) from *Tales of Troy and Greece* (Longmans 1907, Faber and Faber 1957.)
Naomi Lewis	'Baucis and Philemon'*
Christopher Martin	'The Tragic Story of Antigone'* (based on Sophocles)

13

Dr. William Montgomerie	'The Golden Ass'* (from Apuleius)
	'In the Beginning'*
	'The Wanderings of Aeneas'* (based on the *Aeneid*)
Rosemary Sutcliff	'Apollo and Hyacinthus'*
	'Persephone'*

*written for this anthology

Of the other stories three, 'Apollo and the Oracle at Delphi', 'Hermes, Messenger of the Gods' and 'The Youngest God', are retold mainly from the Homeric Hymns; 'Echo and Narcissus' is based on 'The Curse of Echo' in *The Children of the Dawn*, by E. F. Buckley (Wells Gardner c. 1908) and 'Peleus and Thetis' is in part based on 'Peleus and the Sea King's Daughter' in *The Golden Porch* by W. M. L. Hutchinson (Longman c. 1905); the rest are assembled from classical dictionaries and reference books, not from other versions for children. The editor acknowledges her indebtedness to the books of Professor A. J. Rose and C. Kerényi, in particular, and also to Dr. Michael Grant's *Myths of the Greeks and Romans* (Weidenfeld and Nicholson, 1962).

Acknowledgements

Acknowledgements are due to the holders of copyrights for kind permission to include certain stories in this book as follows:

To Roger Lancelyn Green and The Bodley Head for 'Erigone and Her Dog' from *Tales the Muses Told*. © Roger Lancelyn Green, 1965.

To Rosemary Sutcliff for 'Persephone' and 'Apollo and Hyacinthus'. © Rosemary Sutcliff, 1973.

To Naomi Lewis for 'Baucis and Philemon'. © Naomi Lewis, 1973.

To Dr. William Montgomerie for 'In the Beginning', 'The Wanderings of Aeneas' and 'The Golden Ass'. © William Montgomerie, 1973.

To Christopher Martin for 'The Tragic Story of Antigone'. © Christopher Martin, 1973.

To Dennis Butts for 'The Childhood of Achilles' and 'The Homecoming of Agamemnon'. © Dennis Butts, 1973.

Foreword

Making this collection of stories from Greek mythology gives me the chance to record my great debt to the late Professor A. J. Church. It was he, although I did not then notice his name, who gave me, at the age of ten, an experience which has remained a vivid and treasured memory.

I clearly recall that dull November day when I felt at odds with the world, and wanted to be by myself. Instead of going for 'elevenses' and out into the gravel playground with the rest of the Juniors, at the mid-morning break I wandered into the nearby Senior Classroom. This was strictly against the Rules. There, on the desks, were books the girls were to study in the next lesson. Being an unsatisfied and greedy reader, and ready to try anything, naturally I opened one of the books. The illustrations, utterly unlike anything I had seen before, and on shiny pinkish paper, were mostly of men in helmets fighting on foot or in horse-drawn chariots. I began to read. If the pictures were strange the writing was even more so, but I had hardly begun to make sense of what I read before, summoned by the bell, I had to return to my own classroom. However, I was excited by that book. I went back secretly each day until I had read it all.

Re-reading *The Story of the Iliad* I realize, more than ever, my good fortune in coming across the book as and when I did. I still think Church is grand, grand in language and in vision. He never explains and is not always easy to understand, but his concise heroic style can be, for the young, a glorious introduction to Homer. Church, in his retelling, does not reduce the drama of the story nor minimize the savage brutality of the fighting and yet he includes all those details (often left out of later retellings) that build up a picture in the mind. He chooses from Homer's similes those which are effective and memorable, and knows exactly what touches of realism to keep. One small personal peculiarity is that although other names are in their Greek form Church used 'Ulysses' from the first.

The extract (or more accurately, an assembling of extracts) taken from the *Iliad* for my anthology does stand apart from the rest of the collection because of the language, sentence structure and heroic tone. And there is, too, considerable difference in style amongst the other stories—natural enough when authors are so far separated in time as, say, Lamb and Naomi Lewis and Charles Kingsley and Rosemary Sutcliff. But this lack of uniformity may help rather than hinder children in their further reading, for among the books of Greek and Roman mythology now in print and available to them, there is little similarity in style and treatment, while, very often, there are factual differences in versions of the same story. Not surprisingly, of course, since there are as many local variants of these ancient tales as in the legends and folklore of other countries. But my point is that in, say, four books of Greek myths and hero tales there will be differences in details of plot (compare the account of Theseus and Ariadne, for example, in Lang, Colum and James Reeves) as well as variety in treatment and presentation almost as great as the differences in style in this collection of stories by different hands where, despite the range in period, there is consistency in the attitude of the reteller.

It may be interesting here to give in outline an historical survey of the noteworthy editions for children of the classic myths and legends. Charles Lamb's *The Adventures of Ulysses* (1808: based on Chapman's translation of Homer) is one of the earliest to survive. Lamb wrote in defiance of those moralists of his day who had 'banished' fairy tales and other imaginative literature 'from the nursery'. There is freshness and a youthful excitement in Lamb's narrative, almost as though he were recounting personal experience and not a tale of long ago. He described the *Odyssey*, in his Preface, as: the story of 'a brave man struggling with adversity, who with inimitable presence of mind forces a way for himself through the severest trials to which human life can be exposed; striving against external forces or internal temptations, the twofold danger which a wise fortitude must expect to encounter in its course through this world'.

F. J. Harvey Darton *(Children's Books in England)* writes 'Lamb achieved the strange feat of getting some of the *Odyssey's* glorious ease into what might almost be simple Elizabethan prose'.

When the American novelist, Nathaniel Hawthorne, sat down in the summer of 1851 to write the Greek 'baby stories' (which as he wrote he tried out on his eight-year-old daughter and five-year-old son) he was concerned about making the 'old legends so brimming over with everything that is abhorrent to our Christianized moral sense' suitable for children. The immediate popularity of his very free retellings in *A Wonder Book* (1851) and *Tanglewood Tales* (1853), owe their continued success with children to his art as novelist and storyteller, but little remains in these much embellished tales of the native tone and atmosphere of Greek mythology. Hawthorne turns Pandora and Epimetheus, Europa and her brothers, and Proserpina into children and takes the details of food and suchlike from his own time. In *A Wonder Book* he creates a house-party of children to hear the tales told aloud, and the invitation to listen, in one instance is, 'be still as so many mice . . . and I shall tell you a sweet, pretty story of a gorgon's head.' The books soon became children's 'classics' in their own right, and are still available in several editions.

Thomas Bulfinch, another American, writing to 'popularize mythology' and not specifically for young people, produced *The Age of Fable* in 1855. He left out everything 'offensive to pure taste and good morals', and linked his tremendous coverage of classical myths (including also Norse myths and the Druids) to English and American poets. Since his sources are mainly Virgil and Ovid, he uses the Latin versions of Greek names. *The Age of Fable,* which has a full Index to characters, places and occasional subjects, a neat little list of Proverbial Expressions, and detailed chapter headings, became a reference book of world-wide repute.

The year after Bulfinch's *Age of Fable* appeared in the United States, *The Heroes* by Charles Kingsley was published in England. This consists of full accounts of Perseus, The Argonauts and Theseus, and for many years remained *the* classic retelling. Even today Kingsley's flowing and balanced prose seems 'right' for these heroic legends, and no other more recent versions (with the possible exception of Lang) give them in such detail. Kingsley was a scholar with an extensive knowledge of Greek literature, but he was also a man of his time. Although enraged, so I have been told, by Hawthorne's 'prettifying', he, as author, intrudes as Hawthorne did into the storytelling, addressing his readers, sometimes making comments and even moralizing. But this does not reduce the importance of his work. Children today may well become enthralled by *The Heroes* if they have the book at the right time, or, happily, hear it read aloud.

Since Kingsley's attitude towards Greek mythology and the heroes was so different from Hawthorne's, quite as different as the way in which each told the same story, it is astonishing that their names should be bracketed even today when retellings for children are discussed.

The classical writings of the Reverend A. J. Church (1829–1912), schoolmaster, and sometime Professor of Latin at University College, London, seem to have made little impression beyond his own time. He has no standing as an authority, is seldom referred to and is not included in the Oxford Companions to English and Classical Literature. Yet his *Story of the Iliad* (1891), surely one of the earliest retellings, is still one of the liveliest, in that it keeps, in conversations and asides, Homer's indications of personality, the little descriptions of life, with details of family relationships and of man and master, of food, habits and customs, that make the characters more real than they are, in spite of inserted explanations, in many more recent retellings. Those of his books that come within this brief summary were all published between 1878 and 1898 (Seeley & Co. London, with illustrations after Flaxman) and none are now in print. But in 1905–7, when he was in his late seventies, he rewrote *The Story of the Aeneid, The Story of the Iliad* and *The Story of the Odyssey* in a simpler style for 'Children' or for 'Boys and Girls'. It is these versions which have recently been republished by the American company which included them in a series of Children's Classics more than thirty years ago.

Andrew Lang, already known for his share in translations from Homer [with Butcher (1879) and Leaf & Myers (1883)] and as Editor of the Colour fairy books and other collections of stories for children, in 1907 produced *Tales of Troy and Greece* and showed himself to be a superb if slightly over-romantic storyteller. He followed Kingsley in using several sources, 'invented a point or two where the old Greek poems are lost', and manipulated his material in an original way. He is the only one, so far as I know, to give the complete story of Athamas and Nephele and of Ino's treatment of her step-children, although several sources hint at the 'Hop o' my Thumb' plot. (It appears in this collection as 'Helle and Phrixus'.)

At the same time that the important retellings of Kingsley, Church and Lang were published, and for some years afterwards, there was a proliferation on both sides of the Atlantic of books for children of the Greek and Roman myths. Every conceivable source seems to have been used and the *Metamorphoses* of Ovid and the *Age of Fable* thoroughly combed, for never since have so many major and minor stories been retold. Some were good, many more were insipid with little relation to their origins.

Two writers whose books appeared early (at the same time as Church's children's versions) and lasted well into the twenties were W. M. L. Hutchinson and E. F. Buckley. Their work did not overlap, but they used the Greek and Latin poets as sources and both belonged to the 'poetic' and emotional school of writing, inventing a good deal in the way of background and conversation.

In Part I of *Orpheus with his Lute* by Miss Hutchinson the Nine Muses look on the young Orpheus as their 'fosterling and pupil', and tell him, on successive nights in a moonlit forest glade, about the creation of the world and the coming of the gods, about the Firebringer, and the Flood, and Demeter and Coré and other stories. The ninth story is Calliope's, and when it is finished she says: ' "And now, dear one, you have heard the last of our nine wonder-stories . . . but tonight there must be no sadness of farewell . . . Lean your little head on my shoulder—and we will sing you to sleep." So Orpheus rested in her tender arms, and while drowsiness weighed down his eyelids, he heard once again the song of the Nine as though it were the song of nightingales . . .' Part II, ten years on, is the story of Orpheus the musician (who by then knew that he was Calliope's son), and his winning and losing of Eurydice. In *The Golden Porch* Miss Hutchinson retells such stories as 'Peleus and Thetis', 'The First Horse' (Bellerophon), 'The Lad with One Sandal' (Jason) and 'The Builders of Troy'. (The story of 'Peleus and Thetis' in this anthology comes in part from Miss Hutchinson.) Elsie Buckley in *Children of the Dawn* (1908), tells ten un-related stories among which are 'The Riddle of the Sphinx', 'Hero and Leander', 'Alcestis' and 'Paris and Oenone'. ('Echo and Narcissus' in this anthology is adapted from her 'Curse of Echo'). *The Children of the Dawn*, in spite of its title, is for older readers than W. M. L. Hutchinson's book, and, in its day, had a following among romantically-minded girls. It was also much used by storytellers. Today, the poetical style of both writers seems overwhelming in sentiment. It is, perhaps, difficult to understand the long life (they were being read on each side of the Atlantic in the twenties and early thirties) and popularity of these books until one remembers how flavourless most retellings were and also what a

22

tremendous vogue there was, following Lang's 'Colour' books, for romantic fairy stories. In their day both authors must have provided genuine imaginative stimulus to children by giving them 'wonder tales' more nearly related to human emotions and experience than most retold legends published during that period.

The Irish poet Padraic Colum, writing (1918 and later) in the United States, was also an innovator: he rearranges the story of Troy and the story of the Argonauts to include other material; he invents what is necessary to make his retelling seem natural and enlarges or clips at will. Colum is an accomplished storyteller but perhaps not everyone will agree with his publishers that his stories are 'grander than the myths and legends on which they are based'. Out of print for some years, his two books, recently reprinted in their original format, are now available again.

During the late forties and early fifties in England there began a vogue to present Greek myths in popular, idiomatic and modern retellings. G. B. Harrison in *New Tales from Troy* was, I believe, the first writer to try this method. Aubrey de Selincourt followed in 1950 with *Odysseus the Wanderer* (although he intended his book to lead to the reading of a standard translation); then Robert Graves produced *The Siege and Fall of Troy* and *Myths of Ancient Greece* in 1958–60. Elizabeth Cook (in *The Ordinary and the Fabulous*) describes them as 'short, snappy stories, almost cheeky in tone'.

More recently still, Compton Mackenzie, following his success in telling stories about the Greek heroes to young children on a B.B.C. Television programme, has produced a full account of Heracles in *The Strongest Man on Earth*. Although written in easy conversational style, his book really belongs to the next division, that of the present and contemporary scene.

Modern retelling, crisp, colloquial and non-heroic in style, may not, twenty years ago, have had sustained success. There are signs that this kind of treatment is returning, for never before have so many books been published from so many publishers in such variety of size and shape, and in such widely differing style.

There are picture-books, single stories with many illustrations, collections of stories, continuous narratives which may contain almost every epic and hero tale briefly dealt with, or a selection of these told in depth. And with these new books there have been reprints of older titles. The age-range for which the books are designed is wide, beginning with young children of six and seven through to those in their mid-teens, and there are also productions at differing age levels in the several categories.

The impetus for this renewed enthusiasm among the publishers and writers for children very possibly lies in the widespread interest in new archaeological discoveries which have resulted in the publication of books for the adult general reader as well as for the student.

In this book each story is complete in itself and can be read without reference to any other, except perhaps to the introductory story, 'In the Beginning'. But, although the stories are independent of each other, there is often a link between them, and not only in the obvious sense that the same characters appear. These connections may be slight, merely amplifying a statement such as, for example, that the gods frequently came to earth in disguise, or they may add considerably to the understanding of a character or a situation. Children are unlikely to be consciously aware of any interrelation, but those who go to the Underworld with Aeneas and the Sybil will know why Antigone wished so passionately to give Polyneices at least part of the burial rite commanded by the gods, and, if they read about the funeral ceremonies in the extract from the *Iliad*, they will realize how pitifully little she was able to do.

These links were not deliberately calculated, they emerged, seemingly by chance, as the chosen stories were finished and put together.

'The Golden Ass', oddly enough, was the first of the especially contributed stories to be written,—it came from a casual remark that I thought there had been no retelling since Mrs. Lang's much simplified version in *The Red Book of Romance*, and it influenced my choice of the final stories in the anthology. For when presented with a story from Italy it seemed only logical to follow the sack of Troy with a summary of the Aeneid and the legend of the founding of Rome; thus showing the fulfilment of the prophecies concerning Aeneas and his family, and of Zeus's promise to Aphrodite that her son would survive to carry out his destined purpose.

There are many people to whom I am grateful for help. First I must thank those who gave time and thought to write stories specifically for me—I could not have made this anthology without them: Dr. William Montgomerie for 'In the Beginning' (where he has presented a clear, consistent account of the Creation and the Olympian gods from the varied, often contradictory Greek legends), 'The Wanderings of Aeneas' (from the *Aeneid*), and 'The Golden Ass' (from Apuleius); Rosemary Sutcliff for her retellings of 'Persephone' and 'Apollo and Hyacinthus'; Dennis Butts for 'The Childhood of Achilles' and 'The Return of Agamemnon' (based on the *Oresteia* of Aeschylus); Christopher Martin for 'The Tragic Story of Antigone' (based on the *Antigone* of Sophocles); and Naomi Lewis for her attractive version of 'Baucis and Philemon', from Ovid. I must also thank my old friend Roger Lancelyn Green for allowing me to include, slightly altered, 'Erigone and Her Dog' from *Tales the Muses Told*.

I acknowledge my great indebtedness to Professor A. J. Rose. He has been my authority and my guide; I have constantly consulted the *Handbook of Greek Mythology, Gods and Heroes of the Greeks* and the *Handbook of Greek Literature*. Two other useful books are *Gods of the Greeks* and *Heroes of the Greeks* by C. Kerényi; in these I several times found details of stories given only in outline elsewhere. I also consulted *Myths of the Greeks and Romans* by Michael Grant, particularly for the stories set in Italy.

Phyllis Hunt, the children's editor of Faber and Faber, who suggested a book of Greek tales in 1966, has shown great patience, and I should like to thank her for her forbearance as well as for her critical help and continued advice and encouragement. I am grateful to Edna Lewis, who typed the manuscript not once but several times, and often from almost unreadable copy, to Elizabeth Brommer, who worked on the Index, and to Jasmine Atterbury, who completed it and gave me invaluable help with the last reading of the manuscript.

Faith Jaques's drawings add greatly to the appearance of the finished book, and it is clear from her imaginative and meticulous work that she took personal pleasure in illustrating these ancient tales.

K.M.L.

In the Beginning

At first, before there was any world, there was only con-
fusion which the Greeks called Chaos. Then out of Chaos
came Mother Earth, whose name was Gaea, and Uranus
the Sky who hung closely over the Earth. Around Earth
ran the river Ocean in a great circle.

Gaea produced grass, trees, flowers and all plant life and
the animals that ate the grass and the birds that ate the
seeds of grass and plants. Every beast and creature, and all
that grew, in the hills and valleys and on the plains, sprang
from Mother Earth because of the life-giving rain from the
Sky. Sky and Earth then produced the springs and lakes, the
thousands of rivers (including the dreaded Styx and the
other four dark rivers of the Underworld), and the nereids,
the dryads, the nymphs and fauns, and all the other nature-
spirits belonging to the waters, the fields, the woods and the
high places of earth and sky.

The first children born to Uranus and Gaea were six
sons and six daughters, the twelve Titans. These Titans
were the elder gods, the great primeval deities of nature
and the elements. Some of the twelve were: Oceanus of
the seas, who was father of hundreds of neat-ankled sea
nymphs; Hyperion the Sun, who drove his chariot across
the heavens from dawn to sunset; Phoebe, Queen of the
Night, the Moon; Rhea, who was to be the mother of a new
race of gods; Themis, the wise goddess of Justice; Mnemosyne,
who was memory, necessary for all activities of the mind;
and the cleverest and most important of all—Cronus. The
first Titans had children: Eos the Dawn, Hecate of the dark

27

Night, who with her hounds patrolled the waste regions of the Underworld, Atlas and many others. The best remembered is Prometheus, the friend of mortal man.

Uranus and Gaea also produced monstrosities: first the three Round-Eyes, or Cyclops, huge creatures each with just one eye in the middle of his forehead. They thought slowly, were fierce and very strong; worked with metal and in after years made thunderbolts and lightning. Next three other horrible monsters were born. They were terrifying beyond imagining, for each had a hundred hands and fifty heads. Uranus, hating their ugliness, imprisoned them under the earth. But Uranus was jealous of *all* his children, and wanted them always to be out of sight. The brooding weight of the sky cramped the surface of the earth; there was hardly any space in which to move, and Mother Earth herself had little peace and no rest from the presence of Uranus. At last, and when she felt she had produced enough children, Gaea called her son Cronus and persuaded him to attack Uranus with her sickle of grey adamant. From drops of Uranus' blood which fell on the earth came the Giants, implacable enemies of the gods, and the three Furies, or Erinyes, the terrible avengers of the unpunished sins of men.

Cronus, with the help of his brothers, pushed Sky up from the Earth; Uranus thus became the Heavens, where sun, moon and stars had their place, and Earth and Sky were now separated for ever.

So, the first beginning came to an end. Cronus became chief of the Titans, and ruled as king from Mount Othrys. He took Rhea as his wife.

With more sunlight, air and space, the fruits of the earth grew in greater abundance and more perfectly than before. The world in those days was a kind of Garden of Eden, where the first gentle race of men lived long, happy lives, without sin and at peace with every other creature. There were no laws, for none transgressed. Man had no need to work, for earth gave him food and all else he needed. Fruits were always mellow and sweet, the rivers ran with milk and wine, yellow honey hung in cascades from the branches of oak trees; nights and days were soft and warm, there were no seasons and it was always gentle summer. Men did not die. When they had lived out their lives they sank down into deep sleep and returned, as do all living things, to Mother Earth. The reign of Cronus was on earth the Golden Age of happiness and innocence.

But the chief of the Titans remembered that his parents, Gaea and Uranus, had foretold that one of his children would overthrow him and seize the throne. Anxious to keep his power and authority Cronus therefore took his children from Rhea as soon as they were born, and swallowed them.

When Rhea was expecting her sixth child she was determined to save him. So she bore the baby secretly at midnight, and handed him at once to Mother Earth to hide. Then she wrapped a stone in swaddling-clothes and gave the bundle to Cronus who, thinking it was the child, swallowed it.

The infant Zeus was taken to Mount Ida in Crete, where a sacred cave became his home. Here the ash-nymphs looked after him. The heavenly child lay in a hanging golden cradle and, if he cried, the nymphs' companions, the Curates, were there to dance their wild dances, to sing and make a noise, banging swords against shields, so that Cronus should not hear him. The goat Amalthea fed the child with her milk and the bees of Mount Ida gave him their scented honey.

As soon as he reached young manhood Zeus had the power to take the throne from his father. With Rhea's help he prepared for Cronus a powerful medicine. After he had drunk it Cronus spewed out first the stone and then his five children. They, being immortal, had come to no harm, and no sooner did their feet touch the ground than they were fully grown and majestic in appearance. These six children of Cronus and Rhea were the first of the new gods. Zeus' two brothers were shaggy-headed Poseidon, immensely strong and violent in temper; and Hades, tall, slender and dark-eyed, with the pale perfect features of chiselled marble. Around the three sisters shone the glory of immortal beauty:

Hestia slim and gentle; noble-browed Demeter, with her broad shoulders and generous proportions, a mother figure; and Hera, tall, stately and queen-like. In Zeus himself were combined the grace and beauty of his sisters with the strength of his brothers, which produced the glorious perfection of immortal majesty.

Between those who supported Zeus, and his enemies among the race of Titans and the Giants, there was long and bitter fighting. Zeus was finally victorious because the Cyclops made for him the shattering thunderbolt. When the battles were over, all those who had fought against him Zeus imprisoned in dark Tartarus.

Then Zeus and his brothers escorted Cronus and Rhea to the faraway Islands of the Blest, where they lived for ever in serenity, joined from time to time by those fortunate mortals whom the gods judged worthy of this paradise, where Cronus, the husband of Rhea, was king and Rhea the supreme goddess enthroned over all.

In high Mount Olympus the gods made their home. The heavenly city was hidden from the eyes of those on earth by swirling clouds which always covered the mountain top. Men called the gods the Immortals of Olympus.

The distance from heaven to earth was the same as the distance from earth to the rock-walled prisons of Tartarus. An anvil dropped from the sky falls for nine days and nights and on the tenth it reaches the earth. And, likewise, it falls nine nights and days from the earth and on the tenth day reaches Tartarus.

Zeus and his brothers now cast lots for the division of the Universe. Hades became lord of the dread Underworld, the vast Kingdom of the Dead; Poseidon became ruler of the Oceans and the Seas. His most important temples were in the ports and cities on the seashore. Clad in gold he drove his golden-maned brass-footed horses at such speed over the waves that not a drop of water touched the axle of the chariot wheels. Zeus himself held sovereignty over heaven and earth. He took Hera as his consort and so she was the Queen of

heaven with Iris, the rainbow, as her messenger and companion. Great Zeus was supreme god and none dare disobey him. He was subject only to the will of Fate—that dark, omniscient power to whom all were in thrall, even the immortal gods.

The children of Zeus and Hera were: Hebe; Ares, god of war; Hephaistus, the Wonder-smith, and Eileithyia, who had the special care of mothers and infants. The provinces of Zeus' two sisters made them both beloved of men; Hestia was the protector of homes and family life; Demeter had under her care all that earth produced for mortal sustenance, and was known as the Corn goddess. Zeus was the father of her daughter, who was called Persephone or Core.

Among the lordly ones of Olympus Hephaestus was remarkable in that he was ugly and deformed. Hera was shocked and shamed when he was born. Some say that she would not keep him, but threw the infant into the sea, and the goddess Thetis brought him up. But another story is that as a lad Hephaestus once presumed to interfere in a quarrel between Zeus and Hera; his father, in a rage, kicked him out of heaven, and he became lame and crippled in the long fall down to earth. But whichever way it was, Hephaestus was always the lame god, though he was never denied his birthright as the son of Zeus, nor his place among the Immortals.

Hephaistus had workshops under volcanoes and in caverns deep below the ground, but his great forge and workshop were in Olympus. His works of art—figures that seemed alive, tables, stools and cauldrons and other objects that moved of their own accord, richly decorated arms and armour that no weapon could pierce, delicate and beautiful jewellery for the goddesses—caused even the other Immortals to marvel at his skill. Yet they teased him and, in affection, called him 'Haltfoot'.

One day Zeus had an agonising headache. He shouted, 'Come here, Hephaestus, my son. Do what you can to relieve this agony. My head seems about to burst!' Hephaestus took his axe and with one blow split open the head of Zeus. Out sprang the goddess Athene, fully armed, waving her spear and shouting, So terrible was she in her majesty that the whole world trembled and the sun stood still. But when she had laid aside her armour, terror passed. She then appeared beautiful and gentle. Although as a warrior Athene was relentless in battle, she was also a goddess possessing great wisdom, and the patron of all the womanly arts. On earth her temples were second in importance only to those of great Zeus himself. The Father of the Gods called her his 'dear Grey-eyes', and she was his favourite child.

Aphrodite, the goddess of love, rose up from the sea and came ashore at Cyprus. There the nymphs at once recognised her divinity. They bathed her to remove the brine from her body, anointed her with sweet balms, dressed her in queenly raiment, placed a garland upon her head and escorted her to Olympus. Green grass grew where Aphrodite trod, exquisite flowers bloomed as she passed, and the air was filled with birdsong. When she entered the council chamber the gods rose as one in recognition of her loveliness, and all Olympus

32

received her with joy. She married Hephaestus, and Eros, the little god of love, was their son.

But Aphrodite brought strife to Olympus, for all the gods fell in love with her, and she, uncaring and flirtatious, found it amusing to stir up trouble. Ares alone of the gods touched her heart. Zeus decided to punish her mischief-making, by causing her to love two mortal youths. Aphrodite's great pleasure was to fly in her chariot drawn by white swans through the regions of the world, so she saw much of

mankind. Her first and dearest love was beautiful Adonis, who became her constant companion. But one day he was attacked by a wild boar and died of his wounds. Out of the ground where his life-blood had drained, mingled with the divine tears of the goddess, grew the beautiful, frail, short-lived wind-flower, or wood anemone.

Later Aphrodite saw and fell in love with Anchises, princeling of Troy, who was then guarding his father's herds on Mount Ida, and seemed only a simple herdsman. Aphrodite appeared to him as a mortal maiden. Her beauty bewitched

33

him and he took her to his hut as his wife. Before she
left him Aphrodite revealed herself. Anchises was terrified.
He fell on his knees before her begging forgiveness and
clemency. Mortal men who presumed to live on equal terms
with a goddess were usually punished with great severity—
sometimes even death. Aphrodite reassured him, but made him
swear a solemn oath never to tell that she had loved him
nor that she was the mother of the child the Muses would
soon bring him, and for whom she foretold great glory and
renown.

Anchises must have at some time broken his word, for
their son, Aeneas, knew who his mother was, as did his
companions; while Anchises in middle age was stricken with
lameness. If Aphrodite lost interest in Anchises, she did not
forget her son. In the times of his greatest danger and
greatest need she always strengthened, encouraged and helped
him.

Although Zeus was married to Hera he had other love
affairs, with both goddesses and mortal women, and he was
the father of many children. The Nine Muses, who attended
the gods and sang at their festivals, were the daughters
of Zeus and Mnemosyne. Zeus was the father of the three
Fates, or Moirai: Clotho, Lachesis and Atropos, who held
the threads of human life in their hands. Clotho spun the
thread of destiny when a child was born, Lachesis measured
it, and, when the end was reached, Atropos snipped it with
her shears. The Moirai, being so close to the lives of mortals,
were seldom in Olympus, but the three Graces, also children
of Zeus, were often in attendance, for no feast could take
place without them. To men they were the deities of good
manners and correct behaviour. Their names were invoked at
weddings, and at all times that legal contracts were made.
They were toasted with the first glass of wine at banquets.

All the gods loved where they pleased. It was an honour
and no disgrace for a mortal to have the child of a god.
Among men themselves, however, the moral code ordained by
Zeus was strict, and the dreaded Furies pursued those not

34

ótherwise punished; those who sinned against their families, or betrayed friendship, or broke the laws of hospitality.

Hera was always jealous of Zeus. When she heard that the beautiful Titan goddess, Leto, was expecting a child she was fiercely angry, and tried to destroy her. Then she decreed that no land where the sun shone was to give Leto a place to rest. So wherever she went Leto found no welcome, all peoples were afraid of Hera. Then Poseidon helped her. He covered the floating island of Delos with his waves and hid it from the sun's rays. When Leto came there he withdrew the water, and her twins, Apollo and Artemis, were safely born. On that day a golden glow hung over the island, flowers suddenly blossomed on the rocky soil, and Delos became fixed for ever in one spot. Later a shrine to Apollo was built which became a famous oracle, second only to Delphi, and the island was for ever after sacred to the god. No one was allowed to die there or be born there; the incurably sick and women about to have children were taken off by boat.

Fed on nectar and ambrosia by Themis who, with Eileithyia and other goddesses, had attended Leto, the divine infants throve and were soon fully grown. But Apollo showed amazing strength while still a little child when he shot and killed the giant Tityus whom Hera had sent to torment Leto. Then Apollo took his mother and sister up to Olympus, where all the Immortals made them welcome and even Hera overcame her jealousy. Apollo played his flute, his tall sister, Artemis, sang, the Muses and Graces danced, and Zeus smiled on the new young gods.

Apollo was the epitome of physical perfection and beauty. Called Golden Apollo and Phoebus Apollo, seeming almost to reflect the sun's glory, he was the god of light. Both he and Artemis were archers feared for their deadly arrows, but Apollo's chief pleasure was in music. He was patron of music on earth, and in Olympus often played for the Muses to sing and dance.

Apollo was also god of medicine and healing. He had care

for the shepherds' flocks, and himself owned a herd of famous cattle. In character he was upright and just, and having received the gift of prophecy from his father, he determined to use it in the service of mankind by establishing shrines where priests and oracles would answer the questions put to them. He soon left Olympus to find a site for his first temple.

Artemis, so quick on her feet that she could outrun any animal, found her keenest pleasure in the chase. She became the patron of hunting. She had an affinity with the moon and loved the night-time, and it soon became known that she was always abroad when the moon was full. By nature she was independent and early decided not to marry. Artemis was known to men as the Virgin Huntress.

With Zeus in the High Council of Olympus were twelve gods: Hera, Hades, Poseidon, Hestia, Demeter, Athene, Apollo, Artemis, Aphrodite, Hephaistus, Ares and Hermes. (But Hades seldom left his great Kingdom of the Underworld.) The immortal gods were great in stature, and so radiant in the beauty of their divinity that unless disguised their glory was too great for mortal eyes.

Zeus and Apollo alone possessed foresight and foreknowledge, but all the gods were wiser than men. All had supernatural power to travel great distances in a moment of time, to cause events to happen just by willing them, and to take on themselves any disguise they wished—so that mortals, often unknowingly, might well be visited by god or goddess. They did not grow old or die, and time in human terms meant nothing to them. They could not be killed, but if wounded they shed ichor not blood. Their food and drink were ambrosia and nectar. Hebe and Ganymede, whom Zeus had taken from earth, waited upon them.

The bright path of stars in the sky, known as the Milky Way, was the road that led to the palace of Zeus and the great Council Chamber of Olympus. Along this path the gods and goddesses drove in their chariots when called to a meeting or whenever they wished to see the Lord of Heaven and Earth. Most of the gods took particular mortals under their care.

On earth they had favourite woods or glades or hills which were sacred to them and favourite cities where their festivals were devotedly kept and they were regarded with especial veneration. All of them were jealous of correct ceremonies in their temples, and would punish offences and even forgetfulness, often with severity.

Although the gods each had their own responsibilities, when their interests clashed they would show envy, meanness and spite, and arguments would become loud and bitter. The Lord of Olympus seldom paid attention to these squabbles, but sometimes, like an angry parent, he shouted for quiet.

To mortal men Zeus was the supreme authority whose decrees must be obeyed. They imagined him sitting on his immense throne looking out on the world as judge; holding a thunderbolt in his left hand, and carrying on his right arm the Aegis, a gold-fringed cloak of potent magic, with an eagle either on his shoulder or perched nearby. If, notwithstanding supplication, misfortune came to them, they said, 'It is the will of Zeus.' When people sought help from a god they took an offering to his shrine or oracle, and then made their petition. Usually they spoke aloud, but sometimes they wrote prayers on a tablet, such as this prayer to Zeus, found long after the gods had departed:

> *Great Zeus, give unto us whatever is good*
> *Whether we ask it of thee or not;*
> *Whatever is evil keep far from us, even*
> *if we ask it of thee.*

The Golden Age on Earth had long since passed. Men, no longer content with a completely natural life, had become curious and ambitious. They were learning to use their hands to make the things they wanted. The shelter-houses they had built and the garments they had contrived were now necessary to them, because Zeus when he took charge of the heavens and the earth had divided the cycle of the months into four seasons. No longer was it perpetual summer, but instead there was a time to sow, a time of bloom, a time to harvest, and

37

a fallow time, or period of quiescence. As well as long days and short nights there were long nights and short days, but men had no fire for heat or light. The Titan, Prometheus, who was friendly to Zeus, and his slow-witted brother, Epimetheus, had no quarters in Olympus; therefore they, living on earth, understood what misery it was to be without heat, fire to cook by or lamp to lighten the dark when the day's light had gone. Time after time Prometheus asked to take fire to earth from heaven, but Zeus refused. The god foresaw that such a gift would make man arrogant. Zeus had been heard to say that life on earth should be a struggle; man would become lazy if he could do in one day work enough to keep him for a year. Pestered by Prometheus Zeus still refused, and in anger shouted, 'Let them eat their meat raw!'

Out of his sympathy for mankind, Prometheus went up to Olympus and, entering by the back way, stole an ember from the fire of the gods. He put this in the hollow stem of a fennel plant and took it down to earth. He also taught men something of science and the practical arts: how to drill the ground to take the seed of corn and how to grow crops.

The glow was visible from Olympus and because Prometheus had defied his wishes in taking fire to mankind Zeus determined to be avenged. He would himself send a gift to men, a gift they would receive with joy, but one which would bring disaster to the whole human race.

Zeus told his son Hephaestus, the craftsman of the gods, to create woman. Hephaestus took clay and water, and moulded the figure of a perfect young girl, to which he gave the power of movement and speech. Athene clothed the figure and gave her the spirit of life; the Graces and others decked her with jewellery and garlands of flowers. Aphrodite, goddess of love, gave her beauty with which to beguile the hearts of men, and Hermes instilled deceit, wantonness and foolishness into her breast. Then she was named Pandora, which means 'All Gifts', and she was sent down to earth. Zeus knew Prometheus was too wise to accept such a gift, so Pandora was sent to Epimetheus. Although Prometheus had warned him never to take a present from Zeus, Epimetheus was immediately overwhelmed by Pandora's beauty. He forgot his brother's warning and took Pandora as his wife.

Pandora, so lovely to look at, had no idea in her head beyond pleasure; she did not want to help Epimetheus, or to do anything useful. One day, being bored and poking here and there in the house, she came upon the fascinating jar

her husband had told her not to touch. Curiosity made her peer inside. She lifted the lid and before she could shut it again a whole cloud of stinging, biting creatures flew out. They covered Pandora, and Epimetheus too when he came in answer to her cries. Then they vanished. What Pandora had done was to let out every ill, trouble and sin into the world. Later when miserably she had another look into the empty jar a beautiful little gossamer-winged creature, which had been caught under the lid, fluttered out. Pandora felt a sudden lightness of heart; without knowing it she had released

Hope. And Hope has ever since been man's solace against despair.

Zeus punished Prometheus with terrible severity for taking fire from heaven to man. He was chained to a mountain where every other day a vulture attacked him. In the intervening time the wound healed, only to be re-opened next day by the bird's cruel beak. This torture was meant to go on for ever, but after some years Zeus relented, and when the hero Heracles came that way told him to shoot the vulture with one of his poisoned arrows. So Prometheus was unbound and set free.

As Zeus had foreseen, man, uplifted by the new power he possessed, became proud and presumptuous. He felt equal with the gods and did not worship at their altars or obey their laws. The ills Pandora released, and the trouble caused by her thoughtless mischief-making, had brought sin, envy, hatred and conflict into the world. Men and women became so wicked that Zeus decided he would destroy them. Torrential rain fell and water from the swollen rivers raced through the land. Zeus then asked Poseidon to raise the seas so that gigantic waves would wash over the earth. Soon the world was flooded. Men and their cities disappeared. Only two people were saved, Prometheus' son Deucalion and his wife Pyrrha (who were now members of the human race). Warned by his father, Deucalion had built an ark and in this they escaped. Their boat floated on the flood and finally came to rest on Mount Parnassus. When the floods subsided they stepped out and found themselves alone in an empty world.

Then from a shrine on a rocky mountain ledge, the voice of Themis came to them, bidding them throw the bones of their mother over their shoulders. At first they were shocked, thinking that the words meant exactly what they said. Then they guessed that their mother was 'Mother Earth', and threw stones over their shoulders as they went down the mountainside. The stones thrown by Deucalion became men, and the stones thrown by Pyrrha became women. The earth had people once more.

The eldest son of Pyrrha and Deucalion was Hellen, from whom the Greeks took their name, the Hellenes. Thus, after all these beginnings, we are back at another beginning, the beginning of the Greeks who told these stories.

Persephone

Demeter was the goddess of the corn and of all growing things. Without her care the barley could not ripen, nor the trees put out new leaf in springtime, nor the flowers bloom. And in her task of tending and renewing sweet pastures and bringing green life out of bare rocks, she was aided by her daughter, Persephone, whose other name was Core, the Maiden. Their favourite place on earth was in Sicily.

Now when she was free to please herself, Persephone's greatest joy was to accompany her friends the nymphs; to wander through the fields picking flowers, and to dance or sing or to while away the time with them in play in the green meadows near the hill-town of Enna. One day she sat with a gay company of her friends weaving garlands of hyacinths and wild lavender and dark-eyed anemones, the bees droning in the asphodel all about them, and the cloud shadows drifting across the sunlit mountain slopes. It seemed to them that one of the shadows was darker than the rest. But it was not until it was almost upon them, sweeping nearer over the grass, that they saw it was no cloud shadow at all, but Hades, Lord of the Underworld, driving his dark chariot drawn by four night-black horses.

Before his coming, the little company scattered and ran like a flurry of fallen leaves raised by the wind, all save Persephone, who remained standing alone on the hillside, as though terror had rooted her white feet to the ground.

Hades had asked many goddesses to share his throne deep under the ground, where no sun ever shone and no birds ever sang, where the only flowers were the cold bright jewels and

veined gold of the earth, and the only passers-by were the spirits of the dead; and goddess after goddess had refused him. He was weary of asking, and very much alone; and when he saw Persephone standing also alone, with her eyes as blue as the bell-flowers in her fallen garland and her hair as bright as sun-ripe barley, he determined not to be refused again.

Persephone saw the black horses plunging towards her, the wavering flame in their nostrils and in their eyes, and the dark and terrible beauty of him who drove them. In the last instant she turned to run, but too late. Hades leaned low towards her as the team thundered by, and caught her up into the chariot with him. And holding her in one arm, despite her cries, he lashed the horses to a faster and faster pace.

In a breath of time they reached the banks of the Cyane river, and the water rose in roaring spate, spreading far over its banks to check them. To drive through that broad and rushing torrent would be madness, but if he turned back, the Lord of the Underworld knew that Demeter might well overtake him, and Demeter robbed of her daughter would not be an enemy to take lightly. But there was a third way. Swiftly, scarce checking the horses, he struck the ground with his terrible twin-pointed spear. Instantly a broad crevice opened among the rocks at their feet, and down through it team and chariot plunged into the darkness.

Persephone, straining back for one last glimpse of the blue sky, tore off her girdle and flung it from her into the river, crying to the water nymphs to carry it to her mother. Then the earth closed behind her, and Hades, gently now that the fear of pursuit was over, held her close and kissed her and tried to calm her, while still the horses dashed on through the darkness, never checking until they reached the foot of their lord's throne.

In the upper world, evening came, and Demeter, returning to her home, found no sign of her daughter there. She waited a while, then went to seek her. Night came, and she kindled a torch from the flames of Etna, and went on searching. All night she roamed the mountain slopes, calling distractedly like a ewe whose lamb has strayed, seeking its young. Morning came, and she quenched her torch and wandered on, now hurrying, now lingering, always calling her daughter's name, with no answer but the mountain echoes.

Day followed day, month followed month, while in her search, she forgot her care of the corn and the green things growing. At last her wanderings brought her to Greece, and to Eleusis. And here, worn out with searching, she sat down by the wayside and bent her head into her hands and wept.

There, the daughters of Celeus the king of that country found her. They did not know her for Demeter of the Corn, for she had assumed the appearance of an old beggar-woman, for her wanderings. But they heard her bewailing the loss of her child, and took pity on her, and begged her to come back with them to the palace. And when she came, they brought out their brother, the baby prince Triptolemus, and set him in her arms, thinking that the care of another child might be the best comfort they could give her for the loss of her own.

Triptolemus was a sickly baby, and looking down at him as he lay in her arms, pity stirred in Demeter for the first time since her loss, and she bent her head and kissed him. And a cry of wonder rose from the princesses and the queen their mother and from all the royal household, for at her kiss, colour and health came into the baby's wizened little face, and they could see that he was well and strong.

In joyful gratitude Metaneira the queen told the strange beggar-woman that since she and no one else had been able to bring health to the little prince, she and no one else should be his nurse from that time forward. A little warmth and a little gladness came to Demeter, for already she loved the baby in her arms.

Alone with him that night, watching him sleeping peacefully, she grieved to think that, being mortal, one day he must die. And she thought she would do still more for him. She had given him health, now she would give him immortality. Carefully she anointed his little body. She crooned over him the needful charms; and then carrying him to the hearth, she laid him gently on the glowing logs, that all that was still mortal in him might be burned away.

But that night the queen lay wakeful, and being anxious she got up from beside the sleeping king and went to see that all was well with the child.

She entered the nurse's apartment in the very moment Demeter had laid Triptolemus on the fire. With a wild shriek, she rushed forward and snatched him up, turned him this way and that to see what harm had come to him, then clutching him to her breast, turned like a wild-cat on the stranger who had tried to do this terrible thing—and saw, in place of the beggar-woman, Demeter of the Corn, with her goddess-splendour shining all about her. 'It is a sad thing that you had so little faith in me,' said Demeter. 'I gave your son health; did you think, then, that I would harm him? Because I had begun to love him, I would have given him immortality. Now he will be strong and well, but he will die like other men, when his time comes for dying.'

And she vanished from the queen's sight, and went on her way.

Still searching for lost Persephone, Demeter returned at last to Sicily, and one day, sitting wearily by a river's bank, she saw something shining among the sedges at her feet. She stooped to see what it might be, and drew out Persephone's golden girdle.

Joy leapt in her, for she knew that the water nymphs must have cast it there for her to find, and she had only to follow the river up stream to come at last, surely, to some news of her daughter. So she set out again, and followed the river on and on, up into the hills, until she came to a little waterfall shaded by oleander trees, and there she sank down to rest.

She was half asleep when the voice of the waterfall began to make words in her heart, and she knew the nymph of the waterfall was speaking to her, and roused herself to listen.

There were many waters under the earth, said the nymph, in little rushes and falls of water-words now lost, now clear again, and there were waters that ran sometimes in the sunlight of the upper world and sometimes in the dark below; and she spoke of the rivers of the Underworld that each had its spring at the foot of Hades' throne: Cocytus which ran salt with the tears of the doomed souls in Tartarus, the black and sacred Styx across which Charon the Boatman ferried the souls of the dead, kind Lethe that brought forgetfulness of the past to the blessed, making them ready for the Elysian Meadows. And then just as Demeter was growing weary of this talk of rivers, the nymph of the waterfall told how once, being forced to plunge through a crack in the rocks to avoid the unwanted love-making of a river god, she had herself sojourned for a while among the dark rivers of the earth's heart and how, while she was there, she had seen Persephone, sitting beside Hades on his throne, holding a torch in her right hand and a pomegranate in her left.

Then her voice was lost for good in the rushing and churning of the waterfall.

So Demeter knew at last that her wanderings and seeking had been all in vain. Persephone was where not even her mother could rescue her and bring her back to the light. The search was ended. But she did not return to her old, long-neglected tasks. Instead, she betook herself to a cave she knew of, and there gave herself up utterly to grief.

No rain fell, and the grain withered in the parched ground, no grass sprang among the rocks, and the cattle died. Soon there was famine in the land, and the starving people cried to Demeter to aid them. But Demeter paid no heed; and when their continued clamour disturbed her mourning she vowed that no green thing should grow on the earth without her leave, and that she would give no leave to the smallest meadowside weed, so long as her daughter remained pent in the dark realm of Hades.

Then the people in despair cried to great Zeus himself; to Zeus the Thunderer, the Lord and Father of the gods, who alone was stronger than Hades. And when she heard the people crying to the lord of all the gods, Demeter left her cave at last, and added her voice to theirs.

At first Zeus paid no attention, for he was willing that his brother should have Persephone as queen, but at last he grew weary of the prayers and lamentations that beat like waves about his throne, and he yielded in part. If Persephone had eaten nothing of the food of the dead, if not one morsel had passed her lips during the whole time that she had been in the Underworld, then she should be free to leave her dark husband's side, and her mother might fetch her back to the sunlight and the world of the living.

Demeter, full of joy, hurried to Avernus, the Gateway of the Underworld, past Cerberus the three-headed dog who guarded it, and who, knowing the decree of Zeus, crouched down to let her by; on and on through the dark until she came to the throne of Hades and saw her daughter beside him with a lighted torch in her right hand, a pomegranate in her left, while the whispering spirits of the dead drifted by.

But when she started forward with outstretched hands to clasp her daughter as she stepped down from the throne— dark Hades sitting there unmoving with face turned away— one of the spirits cried out that the queen had eaten six pomegranate seeds that very day.

Then a great stillness fell upon the whispering and drifting throng, and all the spirits looked towards the queen. And Demeter with her pleading hands still outstretched and empty, asked, 'My daughter, is this true?' And Hades turned his face and asked, 'My wife, is this true?' And Persephone said, looking straight before her at neither one of them, 'My mother, and my lord, this is true.'

Then Demeter broke into a wild wailing, and the sound of it reached the upper air, and the people heard it and began to wail also, and to lament and cry to Zeus as before.

Now, by all the laws of the gods, Persephone, having tasted food in the Kingdom of the Dead, was lost for ever to the world above. But great Zeus had pity. He gave judgement that for every pomegranate seed, Persephone must abide a month in the Underworld with Hades her husband, but that for the rest of the year she might return to her mother and her friends in the upper air.

Then Persephone laid aside the torch and the pomegranate and set her hand in her mother's, and together they returned to the world of men. But as she went, Persephone looked back towards her dark lord, sitting solitary on his throne.

As they came forth from Avernus the skies were blue and the grass sprang under their feet, flowers unfurled their petals and all the green earth rang with birdsong. And joyfully and tenderly Demeter returned to her old tasks again. The corn ripened and the grazing grew rich and the cattle bore their young.

But when the six months of the year that Persephone might spend on earth were over, and it was time for her to return to Hades in the Underworld and take again her place beside him, the earth turned cold and grey; and Demeter retired again to her cave and sadly waited until it was time for Persephone to come back to her.

And so it was from that time forward. Once in every year Persephone stepped out from the shadows into the world of the living, and men's hearts grew light and they said to each other, 'Look! It is Spring!' Once in every year she left them to return to her lord in the shadows, and they said to each other, 'It grows cold and dark. Winter has come again.'

Apollo and the Oracle at Delphi

Golden Apollo, the glorious son of Zeus and Leto, descended from Olympus to find a suitable place for his temple and his dwelling-place. Over the length and breadth of Greece he travelled, looking for a secluded wooded grove. At last he came to Delphi. On a shelved valley above the Gulf of Corinth on the slopes of Mount Parnassus, there were the ruins of an ancient shrine. Themis, the Titan goddess, who had nurtured him at birth, directed Apollo to it, for it had once been hers, and now, although it was neglected and overgrown, she wished the young god to establish himself there. So here beside the stream of Castalia, nearly two thousand feet above the sea, Apollo chose the site for his oracle.

But before he could plan his shrine, he had first to deal with a mighty, monstrous dragon, Python, which had made this place its home, coiling its huge length around the springs of the river. It ravaged the countryside and terrified the people.

There was a fierce battle, the dragon lashing its tail in fury and passion and pain, but the god at last killed it with a deadly arrow from his bow. When the putrefied flesh of the dragon had been taken away Apollo cleansed the ground and built his temple. To celebrate his victory over the gigantic creature he instituted the Pythian Games, to be held every eighth year, and, since he was the god of music, there were contests of music as well as athletics. The prize was a wreath of green leaves.

Once his earthly dwelling-place and shrine had been

established Apollo's next thought was for priests to serve him. He saw in the distance a ship bringing merchants from Crete. Assuming the shape of a dolphin, the god dived into the sea, swam to the ship and leapt on deck. Terrified sailors watched the sprawling, ungainly creature take the helm and steer towards the shore. Apollo brought the ship to Crisa, the port of Delphi, and then he sprang, as a gleaming star, straight from the ship into his temple. From there the god came forth, to the amazement of the Cretans, in the form of a glorious youth, and began to teach them their duties as priests—the servants and guardians of his altars and oracle. The god's new servants were at first fearful of being alone in such a remote and rocky wilderness. But almost at once the mountain paths which led up to the temple were crowded with pilgrims coming to worship Apollo and to find answers to their troubles through his oracle. The god himself was often at Delphi, and came there in a golden chariot drawn by swans.

Apollo took no wife from among the Immortals of Olympus. He had many love affairs on earth but these were rarely successful and happy. His first love was the naiad Daphne. She was a follower of his sister Artemis, and had no wish for·lovers. She fled from him in spite of his pleading: 'Do not run from me, Daphne, I am no enemy, I love you.' But though she ran faster than the wind the god overtook her, and caught her in his arms. She cried aloud to Zeus for deliverance. The Father of the gods answered her prayer and turned her into a laurel tree. Then Apollo, embracing the tree, said, 'Since you will not be my bride you will at least be my sacred tree, and you shall provide the never-fading crown of glory.' And so the 'laurel crown' became for ever the symbol of distinguished achievement.

Then Apollo wooed the beautiful Coronis, daughter of a Thessalian prince, and was awaiting the birth of their child when he learned that she had been unfaithful to him. The goddess Artemis, jealous of her divine brother's honour, sought out Coronis and killed her with one shot from her bow. At the funeral pyre Apollo, now overcome with remorse, suddenly appeared and snatched the yet unborn child from the flames. He carried the infant to Chiron, the wise king of the Centaurs (the Centaurs were half horse and half man) who undertook his education and upbringing.

Asclepius inherited his divine father's gift of healing and Chiron, knowledgeable himself in the art of medicine, taught the youth all he knew that would benefit mankind. Asclepius became renowned as a physician and surgeon, but he did not live long to enjoy his fame. Hippolytus, son of Theseus, was a favourite of Artemis. When the youth died tragically, Artemis entreated Asclepius to restore him to life. Yielding at last to her pleading, Asclepius exerted his skill to the utmost and succeeded in bringing the young man back from death, but Zeus, who would not allow this interference with the established laws of nature, immediately slew Asclepius with a thunderbolt.

Apollo dare not vent his anger on his great father, but, furious at the death of his brilliant mortal son, he seized his bow and shot the Cyclops who had made the thunderbolt. By killing the Cyclops Apollo became guilty of bloodshed within his own divine clan, and, although an immortal god, he had to suffer the punishment pronounced by Zeus that he was to be the slave of a mortal for a year. So Apollo became the serf and herdsman of Admetus, King of Pherae. Admetus was a just and kindly man, and when his cattle throve and increased amazingly under the care of his mysterious slave he not only thanked him but treated him still more generously. In return Apollo helped Admetus to win his bride Alcestis, and after his blood-guilt had been purged and he returned to Olympus, the god ever kept love in his heart for Admetus.

One day in his travels on earth, in the woods of Mount Pelion, Apollo came across an extraordinary sight. Cyrene, a young huntress, was wrestling, alone and unarmed, with a lion. Apollo watched astounded—then suddenly his admiration for the girl's strength and bravery turned to love. He seized

Cyrene, placed her in his chariot of gold, drawn by white swans, and brought her to the district of North Africa which was later named after her. Here they lived in happiness and here their son was born. The child was fully divine (Cyrene was a nymph, the grand-daughter of a river god), and was given the name Aristaius, which means 'the best of all'. He became a much-loved country god, who gave men joy and many material benefits. He kept bees and invented the bee-hive, so that men could take the honey, he also invented the oil press for olives, and ways of making cheese. He taught farmers to lay snares for the wild animals which preyed upon their herds, for he was the protector of cattle, sheep and goats. Aristaius first lived in Thessaly and then went, by order of Apollo, to the island of Ceos.

When Apollo left Cyrene she returned to her old home, a palace under the sea.

In another love affair Apollo had a mortal rival. He had become infatuated with Marpessa, and carried her off. Her lover Idas, the mightiest of men in those days, demanded her return, bending his bow against the god himself. But Apollo who had long loved Marpessa refused, so god and mortal fought. From Olympus Zeus watched with some amusement, but he soon intervened. He summoned Marpessa and commanded her to choose between the rivals for her hand. The girl chose Idas, 'for,' she said, 'he will not leave me in my old age as the golden god most assuredly would do.'

Apollo also loved Cassandra, daughter of King Priam of Troy. He showered gifts upon her, and even endowed her with the ability to prophesy, but she did not return his love and would not yield to his passionate entreaties. Now a god cannot take back what he has given, so Apollo made Cassandra's gift of prophecy a curse rather than a blessing; for although what she foretold was always the truth, it was her sad fate never to be believed.

But although the golden god gave time to the pursuit of love his real work was the inspiration and supervision of his oracles. The shrine at Delphi was famous throughout the whole country. It was not only at the heart of religious worship, it was regarded as the central point of the world itself. For Zeus had sent two swift eagles, one to the furthest West and one to the furthest East, and they flew back towards each other. The eagles met over Delphi, and there a stone was set. It was called the Omphalos, or navel-stone, to show the exact spot that was the centre of the earth.

The seat of prophecy, on which the Pythia, or prophetess, sat was called the Tripod. When she fell into a trance

she was wholly possessed by the god, becoming his instrument of divine utterance. Her words were taken down and interpreted by the priests in the riddling formula for which the shrine was famous. The ceremonies were dignified and impressive, and the prophecies expressed a lofty morality, often humbling the proud and justifying the lowly. It was recognised that Apollo was the unerring prophet who knew the mind of Zeus and revealed it to mankind. 'Know thyself,' his priests taught, 'understand your station as men; do not presume, but bow to the divine will.'

There were other shrines of Apollo in Greece, and one at Cumae on the shore of Latium in Italy. On the sacred island of Delos, a festival was held every year in honour of Apollo, celebrated with music, singing, dancing and sport. There was also the quaint custom of an offering of bread which was despatched from the most distant point of the Greek world, and went through country after country until it arrived in Delos. In the temple on the island stood a nine-foot-high image of the god. To this temple came long-robed Ionians to worship and to pray for protection from storm and rough weather, and many hundreds of worshippers came to Delos on the annual festival of Apollo.

Amongst the gods Apollo was the most glorious, second only in majesty to his great father. His terrible bow and deadly arrows, weapons of war and of punishment, made his enemies tremble, and the guilty quake with fear. But his voice, as he sang with the Muses, and the sound of his flute and lyre when he played for their dancing showed him to be truly the god of music. Because of his consideration for humanity, and the moral code taught in his temples, Apollo was loved, reverenced, and joyfully worshipped on earth, while the beauty of his appearance when he took human form made him the adored model of all young men. As a child Apollo had announced his own future: 'The lyre, music and the curved bow shall ever be dear to me, and I will preach to men the unalterable will of Zeus.'

Echo and Narcissus

The nymphs who were hand-maidens of the great goddess Hera, lived on the lower slopes of a mountain near Olympus. When they were not on duty, they sang and played and danced beside the streams and sparkling waterfalls and in the wooded glades. Amongst them all Echo was the gayest and her laugh the merriest, while in story-telling none could touch her. So, when her sisters planned secret fun or mischief, and sometimes even when Zeus sought other company, Echo would be sent to amuse Hera, craftily to hold her attention with some long tale so that the goddess would forget to be jealous and watchful.

The nymph was one of Hera's favourites, and when she looked down at Echo, her stern gaze softened and she would smile and say, 'Well, fair nymph, what tale hast thou to tell, or how else wilt thou entertain me today?' And Echo, sitting at Hera's feet, would begin a tale. Sometimes she told a new story, sometimes an old one, embroidering it with her own fancies, and sometimes she would just talk about herself and her doings. Her stories and her chatter were always irresistible and the time would slip away un-noticed, while Hera listened and Echo's companions enjoyed themselves without fear of interruption or of their mistress's anger.

But at last the black day of reckoning came when Hera found out the trick Echo had so often played upon her, and the fire of her wrath flashed forth like lightning.

'The gift with which thou hast deceived me shall be thine no more,' she cried. 'Henceforward thou shalt be dumb till someone else hath spoken, and then, even if thou wilt, thou

56

shalt not hold thy tongue, but must needs repeat the last words thou hast heard.'

'Alas! Alas!' cried the nymphs in chorus.

'Alas! Alas!' cried Echo after them, and could say no more, though she longed to speak to Hera and to beg her forgiveness. And so it was that Echo's voice became useless to her. She could not speak when she would and yet she was compelled to say what others put into her mouth, whether she wished it or no. She left the happy groves where her sisters still played, and retreated, sorrowful and lonely, to the high forest slopes of the mountain.

Now, it chanced one day that a youth, named Narcissus, became separated from his companions in the hunt, and when he tried to find them he only wandered further into deep woods on the mountainside. He was in the bloom of young manhood, and fair as a flower in spring. But, though his face was smooth, and soft as any maiden's, his heart was hard as steel. When he was born, the blind seer Teiresias had made a strange prophecy concerning him. 'So long as he knows not himself he shall live and be happy.'

Narcissus grew up seeking nothing but his own pleasure; and because he was so handsome that all who saw him loved him, he found it easy to get from others what he would. Although he was loved by many youths and by many maidens he spurned them all, and himself knew nothing of love, and therefore but little of grief; for love at the best brings joy and sorrow hand in hand, and if unreturned, it brings only pain.

When Echo saw Narcissus wandering alone through the woods, she fell in love with him and followed him wherever he went, hiding behind the trees and rocks so that he should not see her. At last, when he found he had really lost his way, he began to shout for his companions. 'Ho, there! Where are you?' he cried.

'Where are you?' answered Echo.

At the sound of her voice, Narcissus stopped and listened, but he heard nothing more. Then he called again.

57

'I am here in the wood—Narcissus.'

'In the wood—Narcissus,' said she.

'Come hither,' he cried.

'Come hither,' she answered.

Wondering at the strange voice which answered him, he looked all about, but could see no one.

'Are you close at hand?' he asked.

'Close at hand,' answered Echo.

Wondering the more at seeing no one, he went forward in the direction of the voice. Echo, when she found he was coming towards her, fled further, so that when next he called,

her voice sounded far away. But wherever she was, he still followed, and she saw that she could not escape; for if he called, she had to answer, and so brought him to her hiding-place. By now they had come to an opening in the trees, where the green sloped down to a clear pool in the hollow. Here by the margin of the water she stood, with her back to the tall, nodding bulrushes, and as Narcissus came out of the trees she wrung her hands, and the salt tears dropped from her eyes; for she longed to speak loving words to him, and she could not. When he saw her he stopped.

'Are you she who calls me?' he asked.

'Who calls me?' she answered.

'I have told you, Narcissus,' he said.

'Narcissus,' she cried, and held out her arms to him.

'Who are you?' he asked.

'Who are you?' said she.

'Have I not told you?' he said impatiently. 'Narcissus!'

'Narcissus,' she said again, and still held out her hands beseechingly.

'Tell me,' he cried, 'who are you and why do you call me?'

'You call me?' said she.

Then he grew angry.

'Maiden, whoever you are, you have led me a pretty dance through the woods, and now face to face you only mock me.'

'Only mock me,' said she.

At this he became yet more angry, and began to abuse her, while she could say nothing of her love, and was forced to echo his cruel words. At last, having had enough of this profitless argument, exhausted by the distance he had covered in his wanderings on the mountain, Narcissus threw himself on the grass by the pool, and would not look at Echo nor speak to her. For a time she stood beside him weeping, and then in misery she left him, and went and hid behind a rock close by. After a while, when his anger had somewhat cooled, Narcissus noticed for the first time the clear pool beside him, and bent over the edge of the bank to drink. As he held out his hand to take the water, there looking up towards him was the fairest face he had ever seen. Narcissus, who had never yet known the pangs of love, at last fell in love, and his heart was set on fire by the face in the pool. With a sigh he held out both arms, and the figure also held out its two arms to him, and Echo from the rock sighed in answer to his sigh. When Narcissus saw the figure stretching out towards him and heard the sigh, he thought that his love was returned, and he bent closer to the water and whispered, 'I love you.'

59

'I love you,' softly answered Echo from the rock.

At these words he reached down and tried to clasp the figure in his arms. But when he broke the surface of the water the figure vanished. The youth drew back, thinking he had been over-hasty and waited a while. Then the ripples died away and the face appeared again as clear as before, looking up at him longingly from the water. Once again he bent and tried to clasp the figure, and once again it fled from his embrace. Time after time he tried, and always the same thing happened, and at last he gave up in despair, and sat looking down into the water. Teardrops fell from his eyes, and the face in the pool looked up weeping and in seeming longing and despair. The longer he looked, the more fiercely did the flame of love burn in his breast, till at length Narcissus could bear no more. Determined to reach the desire of his heart or die, he threw himself from the bank into the pool, thinking that in the depths, at any rate, he would find his love. But what he found, among the weeds and stones at the bottom of the pool, was death, and he knew not that it was his own face he had seen reflected in the water below him. Thus were the words of the blind prophet fulfilled: 'So long as he knows not himself he shall live and be happy.'

Echo, watching from behind the rock, saw all that had happened, and when Narcissus cast himself into the pool she rushed forward, but was too late to stop him. When she found that he had disappeared beneath the surface of the water she sank down on the grass at the edge of the pool and wept and wept. And there she stayed, weeping and sorrowing for her lost love until she wasted away; her body dissolved into air and her bones became stone at the water's edge. But although the nymph herself vanished the power of Hera's curse remained.

To this day, invisible Echo haunts the domed forest clearings, the rocky hillsides, and caves, and vaults, and lofty halls, repeating the words she hears, answering when another calls.

The body of Narcissus was never recovered by his companions, but beside the mountain pool, among the grasses watered by sad Echo's tears, there grew up in the Spring, white and golden flowers which spread—a sweet-scented mass—all round the pool, in memory of the fair youth who had fallen in love with his own beauty.

Hermes, Messenger of the Gods

Hermes, son of Zeus and the nymph Maia, and half-brother to Apollo, often made the Immortals of Olympus laugh. The slender, boyish god—the prince of tricksters—showed little reverence for his divine companions, and never lost his pleasure in teasing them. His father, great Zeus, who enjoyed his gay company, used him as his own special messenger. He gave Hermes the official office of herald, to take messages between the Immortals, and to men from the gods.

Among mortals Hermes was one of the most popular of the gods. He was worshipped by the young, particularly young men, whose patron he was in games, physical grace, and athletics; and in rhetoric, poetry and music. Hermes had under his care all thoroughfares—country paths and high-ways—and all travellers and merchants; and thieves too. He looked after herdsmen and their flocks. He was the god of luck. Mortals knew that he was Zeus' messenger. He summoned those about to die and was conductor of their souls to the Underworld, for to him no territories were forbidden—on earth or above or below.

Hermes became famous on the very day of his birth. He was born early in the morning; at midday he played upon the lyre; in the evening he stole the cows of Apollo. All this he did on that same fourth day of the month that his mother brought him into the world.

Zeus had wooed Maia (one of the Pleiades, the seven daughters of Pleione) in her cavern-dwelling on Mount Cyllene, while Hera was unaware of his absence from Olympus. When her baby was born the nymph laid him

in his sacred cradle in the furthermost room of the cavern.

The infant Hermes slept, but not for long. Before noon he stirred, stretched his arms and yawned. Although only a few hours old, he became bored with lying in his cradle. He got up, went to the cavern's entrance and looked out. There, just beyond the doorway, he saw a tortoise. With strong little hands he quickly killed it and took its shell. Going back to his room he made seven holes along each side of the shell and attached to them seven leather strings. He plucked the tight strings with the little ivory plectrum he had also made. He was pleased with the sounds that came from his lyre, and climbed back into his cradle, where he played it. All afternoon he played and sang to himself, finding the words and music as he sang. Then, desiring adventure, he put aside the lyre and leaving his cradle went abroad.

By sunset he had walked from Arcadia to Pieria in Macedonia, where Apollo's herd of cows with crumpled horns grazed on the fresh grass. Hermes cut out fifty cows from his half-brother's herd. He drove them backwards, to confuse the trail, so that their hind-hoofs were in front and their fore-hoofs behind, and he walked backwards himself. When they came to sandy soil he made himself a sort of sandal. Taking small branches from tamarisk and myrtle trees, he bound them under his feet, so there were no footmarks when he walked in sand, and on a muddy path he left only blurred prints. He was in haste now, for he still had far to go. He drove the cows swiftly over mountains and valleys and blossoming meadows. Dark Night, his divine helper, had already passed and it was almost morning when they arrived at the river's bank near Pylos. Unwearied the cattle went into the cave farm-yard and began to eat the dove-soft fine grass.

In a semi-circle Hermes built twelve little stone altars. Then he collected fire-wood, piling it up in a pit. He rubbed a laurel twig until a tiny glow appeared and with it he lit the fire. The dry wood burnt fiercely, and rose in a great blaze from the pit. The flames shot up high and the heat spread far around. Hermes brought two cows out from the yard, and with mighty strength threw them, one after the other, over on their backs, so breaking their necks. He cut off the meat and put it on the fire to roast. The hides he stretched out on a rock to dry, and, so the story goes, there they could still be seen at the time of its telling. Hermes then took twelve equal portions of meat and set them on each of the altars. Eleven were for the Olympian gods, and the twelfth for himself. Although he was hungry and tormented by the savoury fragrance of the roasted meat, he took not a morsel. The gods do not eat the meat of sacrifices offered to them. Then Hermes heaped up in the stable what meat was left as a memorial to his first theft— and burned the remaining scraps and pieces. When all was finished he threw his sandals into the river, and scattered the black ashes. By this time most of the second night had passed and he was not yet home. But just before dawn broke he came back to Mount Cyllene.

No one had met him on the long journey: neither god nor

man. No dog had barked at him. Now the young son of Zeus slipped into the hall of the cavern through the keyhole, like a breath of autumn, like a mist. He hurried on quiet feet to his room. He put himself into his cradle, pulled the baby-clothes over his shoulders, and, with the lyre under his left arm, lay like a little child asleep.

But his mother, the gentle nymph, had seen all. Now she spoke to the god, her son. 'Whence comest thou, thou sly one? Whence comest thou by night, thou shameless boy? I fear that Apollo, Leto's son, will soon be here to drag thee through the door in chains, or else that thou wilt spend thy life in hiding as a common thief. To be sure, thy father hath given me a son who will be a sore vexation to both men and gods.'

Hermes answered his mother: 'Wherefore dost thou scold me, mother, speaking as if to an innocent babe?' He then told her that he was not content they should live in obscurity. Leto, Apollo's mother, had her place in Olympus, but Maia had not asked for recognition from the gods. 'But,' said Hermes, 'if great Zeus, my father, does not grant me the same reverence and recognition as Apollo, I shall use my skill to become among mortals the prince of thieves. In this way I will provide for thee and me for all time.'

While mother and son thus talked together, they were disturbed by the arrival of Apollo. Now Apollo had early discovered the theft of his cows. He had followed the puzzling trail, and marvelled at the marks left by Hermes' twig-bound feet. 'This is most perplexing,' he had said to himself. 'The prints are neither man's nor woman's; nor of wolf, bear or lion. I cannot believe even a Centaur would leave such huge foot-prints.' As he thought aloud in this way, Apollo suddenly knew that it was a son of Zeus who had stolen his cows. In a bound he was on wooded Mount Cyllene, and outside the deeply-shadowed door of Maia's dwelling. All around there was a sweet fragrance. He stepped over the stone threshold and soon came to the furthermost back room.

When Hermes saw angry Apollo he disappeared entirely

under his swaddling-clothes. As burnt wood is hidden beneath the ash, so did he cover himself from his half-brother. He curled up in his cot like a freshly bathed infant just about to fall asleep. But in truth he lay there awake and the lyre was under his left arm. Apollo recognised lovely Maia and her little son—the babe lying there in his cradle, so prudently and so deceitfully. He began to search the room. Many treasures he saw: precious jewels, ivory, gold and silver—presents from great Zeus. And in three locked rooms, opened by his metal key, he found nectar and ambrosia— the food and drink of the Immortals—and robes of crimson-purple and gleaming white, such as are stored in the sacred houses of the gods. But neither here nor in any part of the cavern-dwelling did Apollo find a trace of his cows or of the thief.

He called to Hermes: 'Thou child there! Thou in the cradle! Tell me, where are the cows? Answer quickly, or I shall hurl thee into black Tartarus from which there is no salvation.'

'What unfriendly words thou dost speak, son of my father and Leto,' said Hermes. 'What are these cows that thou seekest? This is the first time I have heard of them. Do I look like a strong man that steals cows? I am a baby who is bathed, takes milk and sleeps. It would indeed be astonishing that a new-born child should go out in search of cows. My feet are tender and the ground is hard. Yet, if thou wilt, I will swear to thee on the head of my father that neither am I guilty nor have I seen anyone steal thy cows. Whatever cows these may have been!' All this Hermes said in a baby voice, blinking earnestly. Then he raised his eyebrows, and gave a long whistle to cover the emptiness of his words.

Smiling, Apollo said, 'Ah, my pet! Thou cunning deceiver speaking already like a trained thief. But if it is thy wish that this sleep of thine shalt not be thy last, then leap up from thy cradle!' As he spoke, Apollo seized the child in his arms and sought to carry him off. But Hermes had expected this, and he brought up a mouthful of food into his half-

66

brother's hand, at the same time giving a great sneeze.

Apollo immediately dropped him, and sat down overcome with laughter. Then he got up and ordered Hermes to come with him. The baby god leapt up and ran ahead of his half-brother, bemoaning his lot, protesting his innocence and cursing all cows. He looked a ridiculous little figure with his swaddling-clothes hanging about his shoulders.

Apollo took Hermes to Olympus and straight to the throne of Zeus. He explained to their great father what had happened, and told Zeus of the tricks Hermes had played and the lies he had told. Covering a smile with his hand, the Lord of Heaven looked severely at his small son. But unabashed, without awe, and quite without shame young Hermes spoke. 'Father Zeus, I shall tell thee the truth. Apollo came into our house early this morning in search of his cows. He brought with him no witness of what he accused me. He tried to compel me to make a confession, and he threatened to throw me into Tartarus.' Zeus hid his amusement at this shameless defence, and Hermes continued, 'Now Apollo is a young man in his prime. I am but two days old. My own father will surely believe his little son and take the side of the younger against the elder?' Once again Hermes foreswore himself protesting his innocence, but this time before Zeus, and not on the head of his father, but on the splendid entrance to the palace of the gods. When he threatened revenge upon Apollo, Zeus could no longer contain his mirth. Looking down at the cheeky youngster he burst into loud laughter, and laughed till the tears ran down his cheeks. Then assuming a stern expression he commanded Hermes to show Apollo where he had hidden the cows, and bade the brothers be friends with each other. Having spoken Zeus dismissed them with a nod, and even Hermes had to obey.

The two sons of Zeus went with speed to Pylos. And there, by the river, Hermes drove the cows out of the secret cave into the light of day. When he saw the drying hides, Apollo marvelled at the strength of the boy who alone had killed two head of cattle. Looking about him he noticed the twelve stone altars for sacrifice to the gods. 'Why twelve?' he asked. 'There are but eleven of the high council of Olympus.' 'The twelfth is for me,' answered Hermes. And before Apollo could reprove him, he drew forth the lyre, which he had carried on his person, and began to play. The sweet sound touched the heart of Apollo. He laughed for joy. By his side stood the young son of Maia, now fearing nothing. He played upon the lyre and sang to his half-brother. He sang in a true and lovely voice in honour of the immortal gods, and of Apollo and his beauty. Apollo's yearning for the instrument was unquenchable. He applauded his young brother for inventing it and praised the lyre whose sound had a three-fold effect: joyfulness, love and sweet sleep. Up till now Apollo, himself a musician, had been able to accompany the Olympian Muses only as a flute-player, and greatly he desired the lyre. He said that from now on the fame of Hermes and of his mother would be secure among the gods. What would his brother take in return for the lyre? Smiling, Hermes graciously gave the lyre to Apollo. Cunningly he asked for his brother's herdsman's staff—and with it he got the care of herdsmen and their flocks. Apollo thought the lyre well worth this gift and the fifty head of cattle. He had now such affection for his young brother that he gave him also simple powers of soothsaying.

The two brothers then returned to Olympus to tell Zeus of their full reconciliation. Their great father smiled upon his sons. Then sternly he spoke to Hermes: 'From now on you must respect the property of others. From now on you must not tell direct lies.' Then Zeus bestowed upon him the title of Herald, with the properties belonging to this office: the herald's staff, the broad-brimmed hat and the golden winged sandals which would carry him with the speed of wind.

Hermes proudly promised to fulfil his duties. As for lying, 'Well,' he said, 'I will lie no more, though I cannot promise always to tell the whole truth. And,' he continued, 'I will look to the safety of all divine possessions. In this I make a beginning by restoring to my brother what I took from him without his knowledge.' He gave back to the astonished Apollo his bow and quiver. Olympus resounded with the delighted laughter of Zeus and Apollo at this new evidence of Hermes' clever trickery.

Hermes was now received into the Olympian council, and occupied the twelfth seat. He was made welcome by the whole company of the Immortals. He always kept his youthful nature, and many times teased the occupants of the Olympian palaces by stealthily taking something they wore or treasured. But Hermes carried out his divine duties with dignity. He was known among mortals for his bright beauty, loved and worshipped for his gifts to man and greatly respected by them as the messenger and mouthpiece of mighty Zeus.

Helle and Phrixus

There was once a king called Athamas, who reigned in Thessaly from Halus, his city beside the Aegean sea. He was still unmarried because none of the princesses who then lived seemed to him beautiful enough to be his wife.

One day very early in the morning Athamas left the palace and climbed high up into the mountain, following the course of a little river. He came to a place where a great black rock stood on one side of the river, jutting into the stream. Round the rock the water flowed deep and dark. Yet, through the noise of the river, the king thought he heard laughter and voices like the voices of girls. So he climbed very quietly up the back of the rock, and looking over the edge, saw that at this point the river had made a pool, and in the pool three beautiful maidens were swimming and diving and splashing each other with water. Their long yellow hair covered them like cloaks and floated behind them on the water. One of them was even more beautiful than the others, and as soon as he saw her the king fell in love with her, and said to himself, 'This is the wife for me.'

But, just at that moment he accidentally touched a stone, which slipped from the top of the rock where he lay, and went leaping faster and faster as it fell, till it dropped with a splash into the pool below. The three maidens heard the splash, and were frightened, thinking someone was near. So they rushed out of the water on to the grassy bank where their clothes lay: lovely soft robes, white and grey, and rosy-coloured, all shining with pearl drops, and diamonds like dew.

In a moment they had dressed, and then it was as if they

70

had wings, for they rose gently from the ground, and floated up and up the windings of the brook. Here and there among the green tops of the mountain-ash trees the king could see them, shining and disappearing, and shining again, till they rose like a mist, and so up and up into the sky, and at last they floated like clouds among the other clouds across the blue. All day he watched them, and at sunset he saw them, far away in the west, sink, golden and rose-coloured and purple, down into the dark with the setting sun.

Then Athamas went home to his palace, but he was very sad at heart, and nothing now gave him any pleasure. Every day he roamed about the hills, looking for the beautiful girls, but he never found them, and all night he dreamed about them. He grew thin and pale, and could not eat.

Then, when he seemed like to die from sickness and from grief, Athamas dreamed a dream. And in his dream Aphrodite, the Queen of love, appeared. She smiled as she looked upon the king and said: 'Oh, King Athamas, you are indeed sick for love of a cloud-maiden. I shall help you win her for your bride, but this you must do: on the first night of the new moon, climb the hills to that place where you first saw the three maidens, and hide in the wood by the water's edge. In the dawn they will come to the river and bathe in the pool. Then do you creep out of the wood, and steal the clothes of her you love. She will not be able to fly away with the rest, and she will be your wife.'

Then she vanished. The king woke, and remembered the dream, and thanked the goddess in his heart. He did all she had told him to do. On the first night that the new moon shone like a thin gold thread in the sky, he left his palace, and climbed up through the hills and hid in the wood down by the edge of the pool. When the dawn began to shine with a silvery light, he heard voices, and saw the three girls come floating above the trees, and down to the river bank, and undress and run into the pool. They bathed, and splashed each other with the water, laughing in their play.

Unnoticed Athamas stepped out to the grassy bank, and seized the clothes of the most beautiful of the three.

Then the maidens saw him, and they ran from the pool in fright to catch up their garments. Two of them were clad in a moment, and floated away up the glen, but the third crouched sobbing and weeping under the thick cloak of her yellow hair. Then she prayed the king to give her back her soft grey and rose-coloured raiment, but he would not till she had promised to marry him. And he told her that he had nearly died for love of her, and that the goddess Aphrodite had sent him to beg her to be his wife. And at last she consented, and took his hand, and in her shining robes went down the mountainside with him to the palace. But he felt as if he walked on the air, and she scarcely seemed to touch the ground with her feet. She told him that her name was Nephele, which meant 'a cloud', and that she was one of the nymphs, who live on the hilltops, and in the high lakes, and water-springs, and in the sky.

So they were married, and had two children, a boy called Phrixus, and a daughter named Helle. The two children had a beautiful pet, a Ram with a fleece all of gold, which was given them by the young god Hermes. This Ram. was the children's playfellow, and they would ride on his back, and roll about with him on the flowery meadow grass.

King Athamas would have been entirely happy with his lovely wife and children but for one thing. When the clouds were in the sky, and when there was rain, then Nephele was always with him, but when the long summer days became hot and cloudless, she would grow pale and thin, and then she would go away, they did not know where, and she did not come home again till the rain clouds returned.

In this manner several years passed, and then Nephele vanished altogether and never came back. Soon after his wife's disappearance the king met a dark beauty called Ino, who had come to the city with a company of merchants.

Now this Ino was a witch, and one day she put a drug into the king's wine, and when he drank it, he quite forgot

Nephele, and fell in love with Ino and married her. And in time they had two children, a boy and a girl. Phrixus and Helle were not loved by their stepmother, who was jealous of them. She dressed them in ragged old garments of deer-skin, and set them to do hard work in the house and fields, while her own little children wore gold crowns on their heads, were dressed in fine raiment, and had the best of everything.

One day, when Phrixus and Helle were out herding the sheep (for now they were treated like peasant children, and had to work for bread), they met an old woman, all wrinkled and poorly clothed, and they took pity on her, and brought her home with them. Queen Ino saw her, and as she wanted a nurse for her own children, she took her in to be the nurse. The old woman had charge of all the children, and lived in the house, and she was kind to Phrixus and Helle. But neither of them knew that she was their own mother, Nephele, who had disguised herself as an old woman and a servant, that she might be with her children when they were unhappy, neglected and in danger.

Phrixus and Helle grew strong and tall. They were more beautiful than Ino's children, and Ino hated them, and at last she made up her mind that they should die. The children all slept in one room, but Ino's children wore gold crowns in their hair, and had beautiful coverlets on their beds. One night, Phrixus was lying only half-awake when the old nurse came in the dark, and put something on his head, and on his sister's, and changed their coverlets. But he was so drowsy that he thought it was just a dream and fell fast asleep. In the dead of night, the wicked stepmother, Ino, crept into the room with a dagger in her hand, and she stole up to the bed of Phrixus, and felt his hair and the coverlet on his bed. Then she went softly to the bed of Helle, and felt her coverlet, and her hair with the gold crown on it. So she supposed these two to be her own children, and went to the beds of the other two children and quickly killed them, thinking they were Phrixus and Helle. Then she crept downstairs and went back to her own room.

73

In the morning, there lay Ino's children, cold and dead, and nobody knew who had killed them. Only the wicked queen knew, and she, of course, would not tell of herself, but if she had hated Phrixus and Helle before, now she hated them a hundred times more. The old nurse was gone, and everybody but the queen thought that she had killed the two children. The king caused a search to be made for her, but she was never found or heard of again.

Now, because of Ino's wickedness there was great trouble in the land. For six long months, from winter to harvest-time, there was no rain. The country was burned up, the trees grew black and dry, there was little water in the streams, and the corn turned yellow and dried before it was come into ear. The people were starving, the cattle and sheep were sick and dying, for there was no grass. And every day the sun rose hot and red, and went blazing through the sky without a cloud.

At last the king sent messengers to Delphi, to consult the oracle, and to find out what should be done to bring back the clouds and the rain. Here the wicked stepmother saw her chance. She took the messengers, before they set out on their journey, and gave them gold and threatened also to kill them if they did not bring as the answer from the oracle, what she told them: that Phrixus and Helle must be sacrificed as an offering to the gods.

So the messengers went, and came back dressed in mourning. And when they were brought before the king, at first they would tell him nothing. But he commanded them to speak, and then they told him, not the real message from the prophetess, but what Ino had bidden them to say: that Phrixus and Helle must be offered as a sacrifice to appease the gods.

The distressed and sorrowful king could not disobey the gods, so Phrixus and Helle were wreathed with flowers, as sheep used to be when they were led to be sacrificed, and they were taken out to the altar of sacrifice at the temple, all the people following and weeping, and the Golden Ram

went between them. Then they came within sight of the sea, which lay beneath the cliff where the temple stood, glittering in the sun.

Suddenly the Ram stopped, and spoke to Phrixus, for the god gave him utterance, and said, 'Lay hold of my horn, and get on my back, and let Helle climb up behind you, and I will carry you far away.'

Then Phrixus took hold of the Ram's horn, and Helle climbed up behind Phrixus and grasped the Ram's golden coat, and quickly the Ram rose in the air, and flew above the people's heads, far away over the sea.

Far to the eastward he flew, and deep below them lay the sea, and the islands, and the white towers and temples, and the fields and ships. Eastwards always he went, toward the sun's rising, and Helle grew dizzy and weary. At last a deep sleep came over her, and she let go her hold on the fleece, and fell from the Ram's back, down and down, into the narrow seas that run between Europe and Asia, and there she was drowned, and that strait is called Helle's Ford or Hellespont to this day.

But Phrixus and the Ram flew on up the narrow seas, and over the great sea which the Greeks called the Euxine and we call the Black Sea, till they reached a country named Colchis. There the Ram alighted, and, now, his life's work done, he died as an offering to the great god Zeus. Phrixus had his beautiful Golden Fleece stripped off, and hung on an oak tree in a dark wood, where it was guarded by a monstrous Dragon, so that nobody dared to go near it. And Phrixus married the king's daughter and lived long till he died also, and a king called Aetes, the brother of the enchantress Circe, ruled that country. Of all the things Aetes had, the rarest was the Golden Fleece, and it became a proverb that nobody could take that Fleece away, nor deceive the Dragon who guarded it.

Artemis, Orion and the Seven Sisters

Apollo's twin sister often left the councils of Olympus and came to the forests of Arcady. Artemis, who had all wild things in her care and was goddess of the chase, liked to spend long days in the open air hunting, or just wandering through the woods at any time of the year, watching the small animals which lived there. She wore, like any huntress, a simple white tunic and carried javelin and bow and arrows. Her glorious hair was brushed severely back and tied with a single ribbon. Except for her stature and the divine beauty of her face no one would have suspected she was not what she seemed to be. But since the forest was known to be one of the favourite places of the virgin huntress no mortal man dared to penetrate deeply into the woods. When the moon shone the goddess was always present; large and small animals danced before her, and plants too and even the leaves of the trees.

High in the wooded hills was a roomy cave where Artemis could rest and sleep. Here she came, attended by her nymphs, to lay aside bow and quiver and javelin, and change from her hunting tunic into soft garments. They ate wild berries, drank from the mountain spring, and talked and sang and danced. Often on hot summer days Artemis and her companions bathed in the nearby lake. They were happy and free from care, for none, save her maidens, dared follow the goddess to this retreat.

Now one day, while Artemis was deep in the forest pursuing a swift stag, great Orion came hunting. He was famous all over Greece. No wild animal, however fierce or cunning, was safe from his club, sword or spear, for he was sure of eye, immensely strong and tall, and very quick on his feet. No mortal man was his equal as a hunter. Orion adored the beautiful goddess of the chase, whose power was greater than his own. Where she went, he followed, but always at a distance. This day, as he skirted the edge of the woods, he saw a glimmer of white in the shadows of the trees and bushes ahead of him. Wanting to discover what animal this could be, he silently made his way forward.

Now it happened that nymphs of the goddess's company had strayed away from the chase, and were resting in the dim shade. They were seven sisters, dressed, like their mistress, in white tunics, and wearing their hair tied with a single ribbon. Suddenly, when they realised that the huge figure of a man was coming stealthily towards them, they sprang to their feet. Orion saw his quarry break out from the shadows into seven white streaks and supposed he had disturbed some rare birds. The nymphs in fright began to run, and Orion followed.

As they crossed a clearing in the woods he saw they were not birds but girls—and, overcome by curiosity, he threw aside his weapons and chased them, and would soon have overtaken them. The terrified nymphs called aloud to Artemis for help. 'Immortal goddess, save us!' Artemis heard their cries and, just as Orion's hand was outstretched to catch them, she changed them into birds. Seven white doves flew up and away from the feet of the astonished hunter. Up they flew, and up until they reached the sky. By the command of Zeus they became the cluster of seven stars known as the Seven Sisters, or the Pleiades.

Later Artemis forgave Orion for pursuing her nymphs and allowed him to become her hunting companion. Leaving Arcadia for a time they travelled from forest to forest and plain to plain throughout the world, enjoying great sport. But Apollo did not think it right that his goddess sister should spend so much time with Orion. He chided her, and jeered at her companion—a brawny mortal with no ideas in his simple head beyond adoration of Artemis and the joys of

hunting. When his sister paid no heed to him, Apollo became both jealous and angry. He made up his mind to put an end to the friendship. So he watched Artemis and awaited his opportunity. He found her alone one day on the sea shore, watching some little fish.

Apollo knew, although his sister did not, that Orion was swimming far out from land. So, pointing to Orion's head which appeared as a dark object bobbing up and down in the waves, he said, 'I shall hit that target with an arrow before you can.' Accepting this challenge Artemis quickly fitted an arrow to her bow, and taking aim let fly. She shot true. Her arrow bit deeply into the mark, and she killed Orion. When she realised what she had done she placed his image amongst the stars near the Pleiades, thereby making his name immortal.

Orion rises above the horizon in the autumn, and stands, facing the Pleiades, club in hand ready for Taurus, the Bull, who seems about to charge. From the hunter's jewelled belt hangs his sword, with the great nebulae in its hilt. At his right shoulder gleams the red light of the star Betelgeux, and marking his left foot is the white-hot, brilliant Rigel. Orion's dogs are beside him and all around are animals of the chase. During the cold, crisp months of the year—during the hunting season—Orion, himself the great hunter, is one of the most splendid constellations of the night sky.

The bright cluster of the Pleiades can be seen sparkling in the constellation of Taurus. When Troy was destroyed by the Greeks, Electra, the youngest of the sisters, could not bear to watch the city burn. In a frenzy of grief she left her place in the heavens. Men saw her go, her hair streaming behind her and her garments a blaze of light. The other six stayed and still make a sisterly group. They move through space together, in the same direction and at the same speed; they might be a flock of wild birds.

The Youngest God

Zeus, the Father of the gods, looking down upon the world, fell in love with the Princess Semele and decided to marry her. She was the daughter of Cadmus, first king of Thebes, and his wife Harmonia, and, since her mother was a daughter of Ares and Aphrodite, and her father also had a god among his ancestors, the beautiful princess was herself of immortal descent. Zeus went to Semele in the guise of a handsome, princely young man and won her love. He told the princess that he was one of the Olympian gods (but not that he was great Zeus himself). For many months he continued to visit her secretly and soon she would have his child.

But jealous Hera, Queen of heaven, had noticed her lord's absence even though the nymph, Echo, had often been a gay companion. When she discovered that Zeus loved Semele she was filled with rage. 'This young girl shall not live to be my rival,' she said. 'I will destroy her before her child is born.' So she took upon herself the form of Semele's one-time nurse, and appeared to the princess as a bent, white-haired old woman of wrinkled countenance, saying she had come to her nurseling to help her and to share in the happy prospect of her motherhood. The unsuspecting princess welcomed Hera in her disguised form. She spent much time in her old nurse's company, listening to her advice and chatter.

One day the old dame said to Semele, 'It is whispered among the people that great Zeus himself is the father of your child. Think you, could this be so?' 'What is whispered may be true, although I tremble to think it,' said Semele. 'The father of my unborn child is divine by nature, for this he revealed to me himself, and truth to tell he is handsome, gentle, noble and loving beyond all imagining.' Concealing her furious jealousy, the disguised Hera said, 'Should you not, for the honour of your father's house, and for the honour of your coming child, find out who he is?' And she went on, 'I advise you to insist that he shows himself to you in his true form as though you were his wife in Olympus. Many a young girl has been deceived and betrayed by a handsome mortal pretending to be a god.' And she continued day after day in the same cunning vein, until Semele came to believe Hera's dangerous suggestion to be her own wish and desire.

'Dear lord,' she said, when next Zeus visited her, 'I have a boon to ask, promise that you will grant it.' Rashly Zeus answered, 'By the waters of Styx I swear to give you your desire.' When the god realised what it was she was about to ask he would have stopped her, but Semele refused to be silenced, and said, 'My lord, I pray you, reveal yourself to me in your divine form.' Sadly Zeus said, 'What I have sworn by the sacred oath of the gods, that I must do, if you hold me to it. But, alas, Princess, you will have caused your own destruction.'

Not fully understanding his words, and made stubborn by the old woman's talk, the foolish girl insisted. Slowly Zeus, great Lord of Olympus, drew himself up to his full height, and taking his true shape he stood there in all the majesty and glory of the Father of the gods. No mortal could survive the sight. In a second, poor Semele withered as though enveloped in flame. All that remained of her was a little pile of ashes.

Zeus rescued her unborn son. Miraculously he both revived and nourished him, and ordered Hermes to take the infant to the nymphs of Mount Nysa. Here, under their care, the little Dionysus spent a happy childhood, in the companionship of wild woodland creatures, and grew into a youth of astonishing beauty. And it was here, on the slopes of the mountain, far from men, that the youngest god came to know his destiny. Zeus dispensed both good and ill to mortals. Mostly what he gave was good, but when men did wrong by their fellows or sinned against the gods, then Zeus ordered retribution and punishment.

Now, Zeus ordained that Dionysus was to be connected only with man's happiness and pleasure. He would live for a time among men to give them new religious rites, and would establish these rites in temples and shrines throughout the world.

To those who had no wish for wealth or worldly power, the worship of Dionysus would give opportunity for spiritual contemplation and exaltation and all his adherents would find relief from wrong in joyful ecstasy. Dionysus would teach mankind to take pleasure in poetry, music, plays and dancing, and show them how to be happy in spite of life's trials and sorrows. And, since he would live on earth and share in the suffering which was often the lot of men, he would provide a link between human nature and the divine nature of the gods. Thus did Zeus order the life of Dionysus.

Dionysus had discovered on the vine-clad slopes of Mount Nysa how to make wine from grapes. This knowledge he proposed to give to mortals: to warm their hearts and uplift their spirit.

The woodland folk—who had loved him since his childhood —the fauns and satyrs, the nymphs and their lovers, the seilenoi—were the first to taste wine. They were also the first to accept the teaching of Dionysus and when he went out into the world they became his loyal followers.

Dionysus prepared for his work among men, and made known the rites connected with his worship. Before he even left the island he met the first opposition that his cult was to arouse. Lycurgus, king of Thrace, came to the holy mountain with an armed force. He surrounded the nymphs and herded them with ox-goads as though they were animals, and then set upon Dionysus. The young god, driven to the shore, escaped serious injury only by diving into the sea.

He descended to the underwater kingdoms and was cared for by the goddess Thetis.

Zeus punished Lycurgus with blindness, and he died soon after, for his impious acts had made him hateful to all the gods.

Dionysus reappeared on a jutting headland of Chios. By the shore of the unharvested sea he stood in the likeness of a young man, one in the flower of first manhood; beautiful hung the dark locks around his head, and the cloak he wore about his strong shoulders was purple. Etruscan pirates in their many-oared ship sailing over the wine-dark sea saw the handsome youth and hastened to beach their ship and seize him as a slave to sell in Egypt. Taking him on board they bound his hands and feet with cords. But no bonds could hold Dionysus, the cords burst asunder and fell from him. The helmsman saw this and cried in fear, 'Unhappy wretches —surely this is a god you have taken captive! Our sturdy ship cannot bear his divine weight. Let us set him back on land at once. If any of us harm him or treat him roughly he will send, most surely, adverse winds and violent storm.' The captain sharply told the helmsman to attend to his own work—to watch the wind and hoist the sails, leaving what did not concern him to others. The pirates now thought they had captured a young prince, or nobleman, for whom they could demand a handsome ransom. The sails were hoisted and the ship's course set.

Then suddenly the seamen became aware of a strong sweet fragrance, and saw in astonishment a stream of wine coursing over the ship's deck. On the top sails a vine hung with great bunches of grapes; the mast became entwined with ivy, and wreaths of flowers seemed to grow from all the rowlocks. The frantic rowers pulled on their oars, but the ship would not move. She stood as still and firm in the water as though she were in dry dock. The sailors shouted to the helmsman, 'We are bewitched, turn back to land, turn back to land!' Even as they shouted their terror grew, for the youth had become a lion; and a bear, standing up on its hind legs,

84

suddenly came amongst them. The men all crowded into the stern of the ship, but when the lion roared and sprang on the captain, one after another they threw themselves overboard; as they struck the water they became creatures of the sea—dolphins. Dionysus, now again in the form of a young man, held the helmsman fast and calmed his fears, for the bear and the other strange manifestations had vanished from the ship. Then, revealing his divinity, Dionysus commanded the helmsman to set course for Greece. Swiftly and surely the ship sped over the water and soon reached the mainland.

After this Dionysus went abroad teaching, and building temples for his worship. Sometimes he was welcomed, but often, at first, he was laughed at. Hera, who had transferred her hatred from mother to son, encouraged opposition to Dionysus amongst the rulers of men, so there were kings and princes who refused to believe that he was a god, and forbade their people to listen to him. Now, many of the Dionysian rites were for women only. Except as priestesses and the mouth-pieces of oracles, women had held, up till then, a secondary place in the worship of the gods. Many men resented this new religion with its appeal to their women, who kept the mysteries of the devotions secret from them.

When, after some years, Dionysus returned to Thebes, his birthplace, he found none to welcome him. King Cadmus was gone, and Pentheus, his successor on the throne, declared Dionysus an impostor, and those who worshipped him deceivers and deceived. He tried to prevent the women of Thebes joining the god and his votaries in revels on Mount Cithaeron which no man might see. But Pentheus was punished by shame and death. He secretly hid himself on the mountain to watch, and Dionysus induced frenzy and madness among the women who, discovering the king's presence, tore him limb from limb. But the cult of the young god was firmly established. Temples had been erected to him all over the world, his festivals were popular everywhere and especially amongst the poor, who had little else that was bright and gay in their lives. Those who derided him Dionysus punished, usually by madness.

But his work as man-god was still not finished, and not yet could Dionysus ascend to Olympus. First came his marriage to Princess Ariadne of Crete, whom he found waiting for him on the island of Naxos, where their wedding soon took place. Crowds of the young god's worshippers, many from distant places, came to attend the ceremony. A procession following the wedding party—horses, deer, bulls, rams, panthers, tigers and lions, all ridden by nymphs—astonished the assembled company. With games and feasting in the evening, the happy day ended in merriment. Dionysus tossed Ariadne's bridal garland high into the air, and sent it spinning up to the night sky, where, even now, it remains—a glowing cluster of stars, the Corona.

Dionysus took Ariadne to Argos, and here he met with his last opposition on earth. The great hero, Perseus, a contemporary of the god's in human years, was also a son of Zeus, but since his mother was a human princess, not an Immortal himself. He had always refused to believe in the divinity of Dionysus, and the success of the new religion throughout the world made him bitterly resentful. When Dionysus appeared with Ariadne and the great crowd of followers, Perseus was enraged. He fell on Dionysus with his sword, and the two fought together on the shore of Lake Lerna. The crowds watched this duel with horror. So did the great gods of Olympus—for there down on earth two of their favourites struggled each to kill the other. Zeus would not interfere to save Dionysus, for he had not yet come to the end of his time on earth. Apollo and Athene, who had helped Perseus before, dared not, could not, aid him now in his fight with a divinity like themselves. Hera watched, thinking her own thoughts. The battle was long and fierce, each gave and received serious wounds. At last, Dionysus, realising how gravely he was hurt, tossed away his sword and plunged into the lake. The surface of the water glowed with the sacred ichor from his wounds, and he sank out of sight. Perseus remained, barely conscious, to recover as best he might from the terrible combat.

Lake Lerna is bottomless. Dionysus sank down and down until he arrived at the entrance to the Kingdom of the Dead. Through the long corridors of time he went, seeing the spirits of many famous heroes on the way, and came at last before Hades, King of the Underworld, who sat on his throne with Queen Persephone by his side. Dionysus remained in the Underworld until he was called by Zeus to Olympus. Having sought out the spirit of Semele his mother, and bargained with Hades for her release, he took her with him to high heaven, and to the palace Zeus had prepared for her. Then Dionysus returned to earth. But this time he appeared in the semi-divine form by which favoured mortals recognised the gods, and in his heavenly chariot. He caught up Ariadne, who was mourning him as dead, and in a fiery cloud, which dazzled human eyes, took her to Olympus. Gentle Hestia, goddess of the hearth, gave up to him her place among the twelve high gods, and retired to the temple of her favourite city on earth. Dionysus, the god-hero, who had lived and suffered among mortals, now took his place at the right hand of Zeus.

Apollo and Hyacinthus

Apollo the beautiful, the bright god of music and of medicine, and the deadly archer, once loved a mortal boy called Hyacinthus, and often came down from high Olympus to visit him. Apollo took delight in teaching the lad something of the arts of war and of sport that he would need when he was a man.

And the boy, being strong and keen-witted and eager to please his glorious friend, was quick to learn, so that the learning was a joy to them both.

One day they went together to their usual meadow near Hyacinthus's home, the field of Amyclas in the southernmost part of Greece, to practise throwing the discus. 'This is the way of it,' said Apollo, and took the great disk of bronze, and whirled about and sent it spinning on its course far down the meadow, so that it landed far off and stood upright and quivering with its flight, cut deep into the turf. The boy went after it and fetched it back to the throwing spot that Apollo had marked out.

'Now do as I did,' said Apollo.

And Hyacinthus placed his feet with care and took up the discus, and tried to copy Apollo's throw. But at the top of his backward swing the discus slipped out of his hand and fell to the ground.

'Turn your wrist—so—and the discus will remain in your hand,' said the god. 'Now try it again.'

And Hyacinthus tried again, and again, and again, until at last he found the way of it, and the discus remained correctly balanced at both ends of his swing; the first time, and the second, and the third; and he changed feet and spun round, and sent it from his hand at the right instant. But it skimmed low and uncertain, hit the ground, and then pitched over on to the turf.

'That was a true throw, but it did not rise enough,' said Apollo. 'Bend your knees and sweep lower, and as you come to make your throw, straighten, and send it upward as the sun leaps into the sky on Midsummer morning.'

So Hyacinthus fetched the discus and brought it back, and tried again; and this time the heavy plate of bronze flew much further before it thudded into the grass.

And the boy and the god looked at each other and laughed in triumph for both of them.

'That was a throw indeed,' said Apollo, 'but rest a little and draw breath, and try again.'

So for a while the boy practised under the watchful eye of the god, and with every throw he did a little better. But still the heavy plate swerved in flight and slightly wavered from side to side. Apollo said, 'You are not putting enough spin on the discus. That must be done with your little finger in the instant that you send it free. Stand clear, now, and I will show you the way of it.'

And he took up the discus and made his practice swings and sent it arching on its way, spinning as it flew and shining in the spring sunlight like another sun.

Far, far down the meadow it landed, cutting deeply into the grass, and the boy ran to mark the place, and bring it back. His face was flushed and his eyes shining and he said, 'That was beautiful! It flew as though it remembered your hand all the way! Throw once more!'

'It is time to be going home,' said Apollo.

But Hyacinthus pleaded, 'This once more, that I may see again what you do with your little finger as you throw.'

'There will be another day,' said Apollo.

'Just once more,' begged Hyacinthus, 'for the joy of today.'

So to please him, Apollo took up the discus that one time more, and made the perfect throw, which it is given only to gods and not to mortals to achieve.

But Hyacinthus, in his eagerness to see if this throw would outdo even the last one, had run a little forward. And it chanced that Zephyrus the West Wind was passing by and because he too loved Hyacinthus, he was jealous of the boy's friendship with Apollo. So he blew a sudden gust of wind that tossed the olive trees into a silver smoke and laid the flowering grasses over all one way, and caught the heavy bronze disk in flight and turned it from its course, so that it struck the boy full in the side, and he dropped like a bird hit by the hunter's sling-stone.

Apollo ran to catch Hyacinthus as he fell, and tried by every means in his power to stem the gush of blood from the dreadful wound. But god of medicine though he was, there was nothing he could do to save one struck by a weapon from his own hand; and before the gust of wind had soughed away into the grass, Hyacinthus lay dead in his arms.

Knowing that there was no bringing the boy back to life, Apollo sorrowfully laid him down. Then, that Hyacinthus might not be quite lost and forgotten, and the joy of the day go for nothing more than a stray gust of wind, he breathed life of his own into his cupped hands and poured it upon the ground where his young friend's life-blood had spattered dark between the grasses, and he drew upward with his hands, as the sun draws the mists of early morning. And up from the blood-soaked ground, under the bright shadow of his hands, sprang a deep red-purple flower, and opened its petals to the sun. And in the heart of each petal, in shadow more darkly coloured, the god traced the grief-words of his lamentation for Hyacinthus: *IA, IA*, Alas!

And from that day to this, the deep blood-red flower with the darker shadow at the heart of each petal has been called Hyacinthus, the Hyacinth, in memory of the mortal youth who had been the friend of Apollo.

A. J. Rose says in his *Handbook of Greek Mythology* that the flower of the story is not our hyacinth, 'which does not answer to the description of its colour or of the markings, but perhaps a kind of fritillary'.

Melampus—Physician and Prophet

Melampus was the first of mortal men to heal the sick; to reveal the cause of secret troubles; and to foretell the future. He was also one of the first to be a follower of the new young god, Dionysus, son of Zeus and the Princess Semele.

Melampus, son of Amythaon and cousin of Perseus, lived with his brother near the town of Pylos where Neleus was king. Good friends and devoted to each other, the brothers were very different in character. Bias was a soldier, a man of action who wanted riches, fame and power. Melampus, on the other hand, cared little for wealth and was not ambitious. From earliest youth, he had spent long hours alone in the woods and fields, studying plants and wild flowers, and watching the ways and habits of animals, and this was still what he liked to do. He was gentle, and his presence was accepted by birds and beasts, and many shy, wild creatures looked on him as their friend. Melampus had himself discovered roots and herbs and fruits with which he cured the sick, for to help men was his great desire. The god Apollo looked with favour on his work and blessed it. He it was who gave Melampus the power to foretell the future, and the gift of divination: the ability to understand more than ordinary men, to expound the will of the gods, often expressed by oracles in cryptic terms.

But Melampus had another gift; he understood the speech of all living things. This knowledge had come to him through his kindness to a family of snakes. One day when he was but a youth, he found the servants destroying the serpents which had made their home in the garden, near the house.

The men had already killed the parents and were about to destroy the young ones when Melampus angrily ordered them to stop. He took the bodies of the dead snakes, and laid them on a funeral pyre and, setting it alight, thus gave the parent snakes respectful burial. The young brood he protected and cared for until they were old enough to look after themselves. Some time later, when he was resting in the shade of a tree at noon, and half asleep, he felt a gentle tongue touch both his ears. Opening his eyes, he saw two of the young serpents, now fully grown, gliding away. As they went he heard one say, 'Well, we have given our dear friend and protector the greatest gift we can bestow on mortal man. Let us hope he will make good use of it.'

At first Melampus did not realise he had heard the snake *speak*. But when he found himself listening to birds quarrelling in the tree above him, and ants by his feet discussing a newly found source of food, he suddenly understood what a wonderful gift the snakes had given him. So he spent more time than ever in the woods, for he now knew what the wild creatures said to each other. In this way he learnt a great deal: for the birds and beasts, from whom nature has no secrets, knew much that was of benefit to mankind. So Melampus, instructed by them, could forecast tempest and storm, sunshine and drought, and explain the cause of blighted crops or unfruitful trees.

Now it happened that Bias fell in love with Pero, daughter of King Neleus. The beautiful princess had so many suitors that her father could not make a choice. He therefore proclaimed that no one could marry his daughter unless he brought, as bride-price, bulls from the herd of Phylacus.

This famous herd was the pride of Phylacus. And it was well known that the animals were guarded night and day, and in particular by a huge fierce dog which never slept. The task seemed impossible. Bias in despair came to his brother. Melampus knew by divination and also from the wild creatures, whose aid he had sought, that Phylacus would give the bulls after the one who attempted to steal them had

94

endured imprisonment for one year. He therefore told Bias he would help him, 'But,' he said, 'it will take time, and you may not hear from me for many months.'

Melampus travelled to Pylake. On a dark night he quietly approached the herd, but as he laid his hands on one of the bulls, the watch-dog sprang at him growling, 'No one may touch my master's cattle,' and held him firmly by the leg. The noise aroused Phylacus, who put Melampus in prison as though he were a common thief.

One evening, shortly before the end of the year, Melampus overheard two wood-worms talking. 'How much longer, brother, must we gnaw at this beam?' said one, 'I am weary of the work.' 'It goes well,' answered the other. 'If we persevere, and do not waste time in idle chatter, the beam will collapse at dawn.' Hearing this Melampus shouted, 'Phylacus, Phylacus, take me from this cell before the roof falls in.' The king was amused when Melampus explained his reason, but he humoured him and ordered his removal to another place. However, when at dawn the beam collapsed and the whole structure fell in ruins, Phylacus was amazed, and he looked on his prisoner with awe mingled with fear. He released Melampus at once and made him a present of the bulls. But in return he craved a favour from the prophet and physician. 'Will you cure my dear and only son from the disability he has so long suffered?' 'I will if you follow my orders exactly,' said Melampus. He told the king to perform certain ritual sacrifices to the gods, while he himself prepared a secret medicine. When all was done as Melampus had ordered, Prince Iphiclus was cured, and regained his full health and manhood.

Then Melampus drove the cattle to Pylos, and having paid the required price (raided cattle was a customary bride-fee in those days) was able to take the Princess Pero to his brother. Bias lived for some years in great happiness with his beautiful wife, lacking only a kingdom.

It happened soon after this that Melampus heard of the trouble of King Proetus of Argos. The king had three daughters who were renowned for their beauty. But the princesses were proud and arrogant. They considered none of their suitors good enough for them. Their own pleasures were their chief concern and they were not willing to give time to anything except their selfish pastimes. So they neglected the altars of the gods and did not perform their religious duties. They had been heard to scoff at the ancient statue of Hera in her most sacred shrine, and they loudly made fun of the new young god Dionysus.

The gods punished their impiety by sending madness on them. In a frenzy they disarranged their hair, tore their

garments and rushed screaming out of the city into the woods. There they roamed like animals, and would allow no one to come near them.

Melampus went to Proetus and offered to cure his daughters. But when the king heard that the physician asked one-third of his kingdom in payment, he said the price was far too much, and refused Melampus's help.

But soon the madness spread to all the women of Argos.

Husbands found their homes deserted, children cried for their mothers. The townsfolk came in a body to their king. 'The physician and prophet Melampus offered his help once, and you refused. Now our plight is so grave we implore you to send for him, that our wives and sweethearts and sisters may be returned to us.' So the king sent for Melampus and said, 'Great trouble has fallen upon our city. I will gladly give you one-third of my kingdom if you will cure the women of the mad frenzy which possesses them.'

'Ah, but you should have accepted my first offer,' answered Melampus. 'To cure your daughters, and all the afflicted women of Argos, I now demand two-thirds of your kingdom. One for myself and one for my brother Bias.' And to this the king had to agree, because of the sad and chaotic state of his country.

Then Melampus enlisted the help of his brother and of other strong young men. They rounded up the frenzied women, and drove them, as a herd of cattle is driven, to a sacred well in the woods. When each one had been dipped in the water she regained her senses and quietly returned home. Two of the princesses were purified in the same way, and were cured of their arrogance and pride. The youngest had died under the stress she endured.

King Proetus paid the agreed price, and in gratitude gave one daughter to Bias (for his first wife was now dead) and the eldest to Melampus. So Bias had his kingdom, and it was he and his children who became the ruling family in Argos. Melampus with his wife settled in Argos too, but the art of healing still meant more to him than wealth. He often travelled to far places to help the distressed and to cure the sick. And everywhere he went he set up shrines and temples in honour of the god Dionysus. Although Melampus had not sought it, fame came to him and it extended far beyond his own country and lasted long after his lifetime. To all the world he is known as the first physician and first prophet of ancient Greece.

Pygmalion

Pygmalion, king of Cyprus, was shocked when the behaviour of certain beautiful Cypriot women brought public scandal to their city and punishment from the goddess they had insulted. He retired into his palace and lived there alone, deciding to do without the company of women and not to marry.

The king was an artist. Carving and sculpture gave him great pleasure, and it was in this way that he now spent his time. One day, as he worked, he thought about the deceitfulness of women, and how evil in the heart could be hidden behind beauty of face and figure. Suddenly he decided he would himself make the perfect woman.

So he took a piece of ivory and began to carve. When it was finished the statue was more beautiful than any woman in the world. And so great was his art in carving that the ivory maiden seemed almost alive, and on the point of moving. Pygmalion looked on his lovely creation day after day, and for so long that he fell in love with it. He treated the statue as though it were really a human girl. He brought presents of flowers and jewellery and he hung a rich gown from its shoulders, and often kissed it on the lips. Sometimes, almost in a trance, he imagined that the carved lips moved, and the ivory body became warm with life; and then sadly he would realise that it was only a statue he held in his arms.

But still, even though she was cold, stiff and unyielding, Pygmalion loved his ivory maiden. He laid her on a couch, put soft pillows under her head and spread over her a warm cloak of Tyrian purple.

Now just at this time came the yearly festival of Aphrodite, goddess of love. People thronged to her temple to pray, to sacrifice and to pay homage to the goddess who, amongst all the Immortals, best understood the hearts of ordinary men and women.

Pygmalion made his offering and, while the smoke of the incense rose in sweet fragrance, he prayed to the goddess. 'Queen Aphrodite, goddess of love,' he cried in his desperation, 'you who bring comfort to the heart of unhappy man, listen to my prayer. I love my ivory maiden with a great and deep devotion. Have pity on my state. Give me for wife one who is in all respects as perfect and as lovely as she is.' When his prayer was finished the sacrificial fire on the altar flickered, and then a forked flame shot up three times. This was a sign that the goddess had heard him, and would consider his request.

Pygmalion returned home. When he looked down on his ivory statue she seemed more than ever to be a real girl sleeping. He stooped and kissed her lips. They were soft and warm! So were her hands and arms. Pygmalion stood beside the couch, amazed, and half afraid.

When the maiden opened her eyes and smiled at him he knew she was indeed alive. Giving thanks to Aphrodite for this miraculous answer to his prayer, Pygmalion then raised the figure that had once been ivory, and held in his arms his living bride.

Aphrodite came to their wedding and blessed them. When their son was born he was called Paphos.

Paphos is the place in Cyprus where the oldest and most famous temple of Aphrodite once stood, and where the goddess's festivals were celebrated with greater pomp and ceremony than in any other city, and where her altars were always decked with flowers and sweet with incense.

Erigone and her Dog

The youngest of the immortal sons of Zeus was Dionysus, who gave the gift of the vine to mankind, and went about the world teaching all those who would receive him how to make wine.

At this time in Attica, the part of Greece where Athens is the chief city, there was a peasant called Icarius, who lived on the slopes of Mount Pentelicus, not far from Marathon.

Icarius was the most skilled farmer and gardener in all Attica. He loved his plants and trees and flowers, and could hardly bear to leave them and go home to his little stone cottage when the day grew to a close. He was a widower, and his young daughter Erigone loved him dearly and looked after him most carefully.

Each morning she would be up before dawn to sweep the hearth and give Icarius his first meal of the day. Then, as the sun rose, he would set out with a spade over his shoulder to tend his olive-groves, and his beds of artichokes and lettuces and other vegetables, carrying with him his lunch of ewes'-milk, cheese and a crust of bread.

While he was away, Erigone would set the house in order, and then sit spinning or weaving until it was time to prepare her father's evening meal. She never felt lonely, for her faithful dog Maera was always with her to keep her company and bark if strangers drew near.

It was to this humble home that Dionysus came one evening, seeming no more than an ordinary mortal. And when Maera rushed out barking and growling at him, he sat down on the dusty road to show that he was a friend, just as any human visitor would do.

Kind old Icarius welcomed the stranger with true Greek hospitality, and he and Erigone set before him all that they had to offer: cheese and olives and radishes; fresh fish from the nearby Gulf of Marathon—red mullet and prawns and tasty squid; and then goat's flesh boiled in a pot over the fire.

To wash down the meal, Erigone rose to milk one of the goats. But Dionysus checked her.

'Kind host and hostess,' he said, 'accept a gift which Athens itself knows not yet. You are fortunate indeed, for the people of Attica will honour you as benefactors. This skin holds wine, which no man in this land has yet tasted. Drink, and you will not envy the very gods in Olympus, for nectar, their holy wine, brings no greater happiness.'

Icarius drank the golden wine, and his whole being was filled with joy at the wonderful flavour. He drank again, and the wine mounted to his head, so that he became gloriously intoxicated and danced as if he were again a young man.

Next day Icarius overslept for the first time in his life. But when at last he rose, Dionysus was waiting to teach him how to plant the little green shoots which he had brought, and how to tend the vines as they grew. For under the god's hand they grew while Icarius watched, and the time of vintage came all in one day so that Dionysus, who now revealed himself, could show him how to press the grapes and make the wine itself.

After this Icarius planted a vineyard and when the season of vintage came, he filled many jars and skins with wine, and delighted and surprised all his neighbours with this wonderful new drink.

So far he had only given them a mere cupful each to taste. But when autumn drew on he decided to carry some of his skins of wine to the village, and perhaps even beyond it over the mountain spurs to Athens.

Leaving Erigone to look after the cottage and the vineyard, with Maera to guard her, Icarius loaded half a dozen full skins of wine on his wagon, harnessed an ox to it, and set out on his journey.

The first night he spent in the village which is called Dionysus to this day. Here all the shepherds and farmers gathered round to see what it was that Icarius carried so carefully on his wagon.

When he told them, some laughed at him. But the rest made a great feast in his honour, sacrificing a heifer to Zeus and afterwards roasting its flesh for their banquet. Icarius then broached one of the wine-skins, and they all drank with amazement and delight.

'This is indeed a drink stolen from heaven!' they cried. 'It smells more sweetly than all the blossoms in love's garden, and surely tastes as if you had robbed the goddess Hebe herself of the nectar which she pours at the banquets on Olympus. Let us sing in praise of Icarius! Surely some god has been your guest and shown you how to make this wonderful drink.'

Then Icarius told them the whole story of how Dionysus had visited him. But by now his hearers had drunk so much that only a few could understand what he said. Some of these reeled home to bed. But the rest broke open another wine-skin without asking leave, and drank until they became mad: for the wine was strong, and they had not yet learnt to mingle it with water.

In their drunken fury, when the ground seemed to heave under their feet, and their eyes could not see properly any more, they became frightened and cried out that Icarius had poisoned them. He tried to explain, but they were too drunk to listen, and they set upon him with sticks and stones, and some with their spades and sickles and pruning-knives; and soon the poor old man lay dead.

In the morning, when they woke and found that they had taken no harm, they were filled with sorrow and regret. But they were afraid, too, lest they should suffer for what they had done. So they carried the body of Icarius secretly out of the village and buried him under a spreading oak tree on the mountain side. Then they fled down to the shore and escaped over the sea to the nearby island of Ceos.

Erigone knew nothing of what had happened, but as the days went by she began to wonder more and more what had become of her father. At last, he appeared to her in a dream, and begged her to seek out his grave and make her prayers and offerings there, as was her duty.

Erigone awoke from sleep and tried to believe that the dream had come only to deceive and torment her, since she was already so filled with fears and forebodings. But when the ghost of Icarius appeared to her again the next night, she doubted no longer.

She set out to find her father's body. Over the slopes of Pentelicus she went, asking each shepherd she met, and each herdsman and each husbandman if they had seen Icarius. But none knew—or none would say.

Then she turned to the faithful dog Maera, who followed wherever she went, and cried, 'Maera, dear Maera! Find my father for me! I fear his body lies unburied, and certainly it lies unwept and unhonoured. I must see that the last funeral rites are done, lest his spirit wanders for ever, unable to enter the dwelling-place of the dead.'

Maera seemed to understand, for he went bounding away. Next morning Erigone woke to find him at her side. The moment he saw that she was awake, he began to howl miserably, and when she sprang to her feet, he led her up the mountainside until they came to a great oak tree. Under its shade he began to scratch, howling still; and Erigone knew that she had found her father's grave.

So she knelt down in prayer, cutting off her hair as an offering, and doing all that was needful.

When the last rites were ended and the spirit of Icarius was free to enter the Underworld Kingdom of the Dead, Erigone in grief hanged herself from a branch of the oak tree.

Even now Maera would not leave his mistress unguarded and alone. He stayed by the tree, chasing off birds and beasts of prey, until there came shepherds from the hillside who had known Icarius and his daughter. They took down the body of Erigone and buried her beside her father.

As they dug her grave Maera helped as best he could with his sharp claws; and when she was buried and the shepherds had gone on their way with heavy hearts, Maera lay down on his mistress's grave, and remained there of his own free will, seeking neither food nor water until he died.

Seeing all that chanced, Father Zeus took pity on Icarius and his daughter and her dog, and set them among the stars; and there they may still be seen as the constellation called the Wagoner, Virgo, and Procyon the Little Dog.

But the story did not end when the new stars first shone in the sky. Zeus punished the murderers by sending such a drought on the island of Ceos that everyone would have died, had the men not confessed their fault and done penance for the innocent blood they had shed.

Ever after at the same season of the year the terrible heat comes to burn up the island, but when it comes, Zeus sends the cool wind called Etesian, the Prayer Wind, in answer to the Ceans' prayers, and the crops and vines grow richly and do not wither in the heat.

To punish the people of Attica Dionysus sent a madness upon all young maidens which did not leave them until an annual festival was held in memory of Erigone and her father. Since Erigone's body had been found hanging from an oak tree, Dionysus gave orders to his priests to commemorate her death as part of the festival rites. Little cut-out figures were tied to the branches of trees, and these twisted and twirled with every breath of wind. And from the strong boughs of the great oak trees thick ropes hung to which were attached small wood platforms. Maidens sat or stood on these platforms, holding the ropes with both hands, and swung to and fro just as poor Erigone had done in death.

But this festival in honour of Erigone and Icarius soon became a happy one, full of gaiety and laughter, where the wine of Dionysus flowed freely and the Athenian girls enjoyed the new pastime of the swing.

The Sacred Honey Bees

When Zeus became chief of all the gods he remembered those who had looked after him in the mountain cave of Crete while he was a baby. In gratitude the great god gave to the nymphs, Adraste and Ide, the Horn of Plenty, the Cornucopia, which was always filled to overflowing with the fruits of the earth, and would give what food or drink its possessor asked for. The divine child had been fed on goat's-milk and honey. Zeus set Amalthea, the goat, in the heavens as the constellation Capricorn, while the bees lived for ever in the sacred cave and no one was allowed to molest them or take their honey. The god had all wild bees under his protection, and gave them their handsome golden-bronze coats and endowed their transparent wings with power.

Once four foolhardy men tried to steal honey from the sacred cave, but their arms and armour fell from them the moment they entered the cave's mouth, and the bees came at them in a terrifying swarm. Zeus did not strike the men down with a thunderbolt for he would not allow the cave to be defiled by their dead bodies; instead he changed them into birds.

Hundreds of years later Comatas, a slave, kept his master's flocks on the grassy slopes of Mount Helicon. In the warm summer months he stayed out all night as well as all day with the animals. He had with him all he needed. For food he ate wild berries and drank from the mountain streams. In the heat of midday he rested in the shade, and slept at night upon his shepherd's cloak. For his own pleasure he made up tunes and played them on his reed pipes. Although he never

saw them Comatas felt there were kindly spirits in the high
woods and pastures. He did not know that on the mountain
were places sacred to the Nine Muses, who often came there
to dance and sing, with the nymphs and dryads of Helicon,
beside the springs of Hippocrene and Aganippe. Sometimes
Comatas thought he heard the soft sound of music, and
imagined the movement of a slight figure in the dappled
shadows of the trees; but that was all.

Then one night when the moon was full and he was
sleeping lightly, he distinctly heard music and singing. Getting
up he quietly went towards the sound. In the clear moonlight, near to a plashing fountain, nymphs were dancing
around a group of slim goddess-like creatures who sang with
divine sweetness. 'How beautiful,' said Comatas to himself.
'Now I know why the grass is rich, and why there is such
happy quietness on this hillside.' Comatas did not know that
these were the Muses, who had come to celebrate the night of
the full moon. But he noticed a small altar dedicated to the
Muses and wished he had a gift to lay upon it.

A little cloud drifted over the moon, hiding its light. When it passed the singers and dancers had gone. Comatas went back to his sleeping-place, wondering if he had been only dreaming.

The memory of the vision he had seen in the moonlight remained very clearly in his mind, and stronger than ever grew his desire to place a gift upon the woodland altar. But Comatas, being a slave, owned nothing. At last he decided to offer a kid. After all, he, and he alone, looked after the goats. He spent his life with them, so surely one little kid might be his.

Soon after he had made his sacrifice on the altar near the fountain, his master counted the flock, and knew that one was missing. Instead of remembering the long, faithful service of his herdsman he flew into a passion. 'You miserable, dishonest slave,' he cried, 'what has made you careless of my property?' And without waiting for an answer or explanation, he shoved Comatas into a huge chest that stood in the entrance to his dwelling, and turned the key, leaving him to die of starvation.

The nymphs missed Comatas and his pleasant piping. When day followed day and still he had not come back to the hillside pastures they sent a moth to look for him.

The moth found no trace of the goatherd in the slaves' quarters or in the stables and yards, so it went into the master's hall, and fluttered from place to place, until at last it crawled over the surface of the chest, and looking in at the keyhole saw Comatas. At once it flew back to the nymphs.

The next day a constant stream of bees flew singly to the chest, and in through the keyhole. They went in with full honey-bags and came out with empty ones. And so it continued day after day.

At last, when almost a year had passed, the master remembered Comatas. He ordered his servants to open the chest, and expected to find the skeleton of his slave. But instead—there sat Comatas, alive and well.

The astonished master and servants listened while Comatas

told them how bees had come to him and built honeycombs in the corners of the chest, on which he had fed, and so remained alive. Knowing that the wild bees of the district were sacred to Zeus, the master realised that his goatherd must be under the protection of the great god. From that time onwards, Comatas, the one-time slave, was treated with kindness, consideration and with great respect.

Comatas often went to the mountain slopes and played his shepherd's pipes, but never again did he see the nymphs.

The Tragic Story of Antigone

The two orphaned daughters of Oedipus, late king of Thebes, were wards of their uncle, Duke Creon, who ruled the city as Regent. The throne had been left equally to his nephews, the sons of Oedipus, but so bitter was their rivalry that any sharing of authority was impossible; they could not even agree to rule alternately—a year at a time. Eteocles stayed with his uncle in Thebes and drove his brother from the city. Polyneices then gathered together a small fighting force and persuaded six princes of the country to support his claim. So seven armies came against Thebes, and lay encamped outside the seven gates of the city walls, prepared to starve the people into submission.

Ismene and her younger sister, Antigone, were miserably unhappy. They loved their brothers and found it terrible that they should take arms against each other. Antigone was betrothed to Haemon, Creon's son, but she would not marry him during such unsettled times. And both sisters feared the future. They knew that a curse hung over the family. Their grandfather, King Laius, in sinning against the sacred law of hospitality, had brought on himself the anger of the immortal gods. Laius had escaped the full effects of punishment, but the oracle's decree of retribution had fallen heavily upon his son, and the life of Oedipus was blasted by tragedy. Sorrow and grief had never been far from Ismene and Antigone. What was still to come? What would be the result of the battle now to take place? Duke Creon and his council had decided they could hold out no longer, and a sortie was planned for dawn.

Count Haemon would be in charge of the city defences. Eteocles was to lead the attack.

It was a grim battle. Heroic deeds were done on both sides, and on both sides many died. Chief of the victims were the two brother princes themselves, Eteocles and Polyneices. At the climax of the struggle they fell in single combat, each on the other's sword. That sad duel decided the day. With no prince to lead them, no purpose left in their onslaught, the attacking forces retired.

Quietly at night they withdrew, leaving many of their dead on the battlefield. When the news of deliverance reached those inside the city, there was great rejoicing, and Duke Creon ordered a general triumph. For his gallant nephew Eteocles, who had died at the head of the Theban forces, in defence of the city and its people, he proclaimed a public funeral. Not so for his brother; Polyneices' body, so Duke Creon's edict ran, was to be left untouched on the battlefield, with those of the enemy, a prey for wild dogs and waiting vultures. Anyone who attempted to defy this order would be publicly stoned to death.

Within the citadel word of the edict soon spread. Antigone went to her sister, 'Have you heard the news?' she asked. 'Ismene, dear sister, have you heard the edict our uncle has had proclaimed to all the city? Do you know the outrage that is to be committed against one we love?'

'During the night the enemy has fled, so much I know,' answered Ismene, 'but nothing more have I heard, either for grief or joy, concerning our ill-fated family, since the news that our two brothers in single combat each destroyed the other. What more is there? Some dark shadow seems to lie upon you.'

'Yes, there is something more. Our brothers' burial. Honour for Eteocles, dishonour for Polyneices.' Antigone told Ismene all she knew, then faced her with a challenge. 'Ismene,' she said, 'come with me and give Polyneices the ceremonial burial that is his due.'

Ismene gasped with horror. 'We cannot do that!' she

exclaimed. 'Our uncle the duke has forbidden it, and the penalty is death, and death by being stoned in the city streets.'

'But we must, we must!' Antigone declared. 'Our religion demands that we must. Otherwise his spirit will be lost, wandering for ever, and will not find peace in the Underworld. Come with me and let us give Polyneices the proper funeral rites. Nobody else will.'

But Ismene drew back, pale and fearful. 'O Antigone,' she cried, 'this is a reckless plan. Remember we two are alone. Our father is dead, and our two brothers. If we do this thing our deaths will be more shameful than theirs. I wish with all my heart that Polyneices had proper burial. But to act against our uncle's decree—I cannot, I am too weak.'

Antigone tried again and again to persuade her sister but Ismene could not find the courage. She wept, and in return pleaded with Antigone. 'O sister, remember we are but women; we were not made to fight against the authority of men. Renounce your wild and dangerous scheme. Do not take this mad duty on yourself.'

'If that is how you feel,' said Antigone, 'I will no longer urge you. You must please yourself. I would not accept your help now even if you offered it, for it is clear that laws of the gods mean nothing to you.' With these bitter words, Antigone turned and left her sister.

As soon as it grew dark Antigone threw a cloak over her slender shoulders, and slipped out of the city through a postern gate. It was murky that night, a mist squatting upon the battlefield. The princess, undaunted, hurried on her way. Past the scenes of fighting she went, past broken arms, neglected stores of weapons, past the bodies of men, seeking all the time for her brother's corpse.

Suddenly, through the gloom, she saw something glitter. It was armour, the golden armour of a prince, gleaming even in the murk. She shuddered. Till then, boldness had carried her forward. Beyond her immediate duty she had left herself no time to think. Now, with the armour glinting there before her eyes and the dim shape of a body, she was afraid. Dare she defy the duke's edict? How could she face the anger of her uncle? What would he do to her? Almost she turned back, longing for the safety of her bed, longing for Ismene's sympathy. Then she recalled the sacred laws

of burial, and her brother's need; her resolve was strengthened and she went on.

Ssh! What was that noise? The wind? There was no wind. A stray dog, a wild animal, a wolf? Antigone trembled with fright. Evenly the sound drew nearer—human footsteps! Not far away, someone was on guard. All in a flash, her desperate courage returned and she darted forward. There before her lay the body of Polyneices.

The footsteps came nearer, tramping.

Antigone, kneeling down, kissed Polyneices' face. With her fingers she loosened soil from the trampled ground and three times sprinkled handfuls of earth upon the body.

It was no complete burial, but it was enough, and it meant

at least that someone had cared about the last rites for the dead, and her brother's spirit would now be set free in peace.

'Halt! Who goes there?'

Antigone scrambled to her feet, as the rough hand of the guard fell upon her shoulder.

'A girl!' exclaimed the soldier, 'and all alone. What are you doing on the battlefield?'

Antigone did not answer, but with her free hand pulled her cloak to hide her face.

The man looked down, saw the body of Polyneices, and saw what Antigone had done.

His hold on the girl tightened, and he spoke quickly with fear in his voice. 'The duke will be angry. You've broke the law. You oughtn't to have done it. Now then, you must come along with me.' And the guard took the silent princess quickly back to the palace.

In the citadel meanwhile Duke Creon was in council with his senate. His rebel nephew had been slain and the attacking army routed, so now there seemed prospect of peace for Thebes. He had been proclaimed king and he was confident. Some of his councillors had forebodings of further disaster, but Creon laughed at their fears.

'My power is secure,' he asserted. 'No man in the city dare go against my orders or my wishes.'

'Do not be too sure, sire,' said the oldest councillor. 'The world is full of mysteries; most mysterious of all is man. Men are resourceful and there is nothing they will not do, if necessity drives them to it.' But the king's confidence was unshaken.

Just at that moment, from outside the council chamber, came the sounds of footsteps and voices. All heads turned towards the doors, and in burst the nervous guard, with his captive.

'What is the meaning of this intrusion?' demanded Creon.

The man struggled forwards. 'Begging your pardon, sir,' he gasped. 'Your Grace, sir. I mean, I had to come, sir.'

Creon frowned. 'Come to the point, man, and cease your babbling. Why are you here and who's your prisoner?'

'Well, sir,' said the guard. 'It's the body. Been buried. Sprinkled, that is, just the necessary.'

'That's enough,' said Creon. 'You may go. Prisoner, uncover your face. What is your answer to this charge?'

Antigone threw back her cloak. There was a gasp of horror from the assembled men.

'Antigone!' cried Creon. 'You?' Antigone returned his gaze with proud dignity.

'Did you know of the edict I proclaimed?'

'Yes, I did.'

'You dared to disobey my orders?'

'I had no choice,' cried Antigone, with sudden passion, and the old councillors shuffled backwards a pace or two in awe of her. Even Creon was silenced.

'No decrees issued by you, a mere man, can override the law of the gods. What drove me is strong and inescapable: my duty to the dead. The laws of heaven are not like the laws of men, proclaimed yesterday, in force today and tomorrow forgotten; the laws of heaven are eternal. What the gods decree we must do.'

She paused, looking round the hushed assembly, and spoke more quietly. 'Of course, Uncle, I fear your anger, and of course I tremble because of your edict. But I am not afraid to die. What I did I had to do, and . . .'

'That is enough,' said Creon sternly, recovering his authority. 'You have been convicted of a crime. You cannot glorify it as a virtue.'

'Then, Uncle,' said Antigone, 'will you condemn me to die?'

'That I will,' answered Creon, 'no more and no less; you shall be immured in a vault and there left until you are released by death.'

'Then why delay?' cried Antigone. 'I do not regret what I did. It was my duty. And it was no crime.'

Creon's anger was now beyond control. Fearful that both sisters had defied him, he shouted to the guards: 'Bring

Princess Ismene here. If I know human nature then she was her sister's accomplice.'

Soon Ismene stood before Creon.

'And were you part of this plot too, you snake-in-the-grass?'

'I was,' said Ismene gently, 'so long as Antigone says so.'

'But you weren't!' cried her younger sister. 'You chose life!' To her uncle she said, 'Ismene is innocent!'

'But I cannot live without my sister,' cried Ismene, 'and Antigone is Haemon's promised bride. How can you condemn her to a lingering death when your son loves her?'

'Don't say "my sister", for you have no sister,' replied Creon. 'And Haemon can soon find another bride.' Then turning to the guards, 'Let Princess Ismene go. I misjudged her. As for the other, she shall die. Take her and guard her well, let none come near her.'

With defiant dignity, Princess Antigone curtsied to the duke and was led away.

The knot of old councillors were quick to surround Creon, full of questions and advice.

The elderly leader of the council spoke at once. 'My lord— you cannot mean to put the Princess Antigone to death?'

'So runs my edict,' said Creon, 'she shall surely die.'

'But, my lord—' he got no further. One of Creon's supporters interrupted him.

'The king cannot make an exception just because she is a princess.'

'And to spare her,' said another, 'is to dishonour the memory of our gallant prince. And it was he who killed the renegade Polyneices.'

'Dying himself at the hands of the rebel,' added a sad old man.

'What will the citizens think?' said another. 'She is the daughter of Oedipus. They loved their old prince. If you kill Antigone, they will turn against you.'

'But, my friend,' countered the other, 'if Antigone goes free, that will be an end to law and order.'

The friend of Creon spoke again. 'Creon,' he said firmly, 'for the sake of the city and for your honour Antigone must die.'

'No, no,' contradicted the leader of the council. 'If the king condemns the Princess Antigone for doing her pious duty to the dead—giving burial to her own flesh and blood—the gods will punish him and the whole city of Thebes will suffer.'

And so the argument went back and forth, till Creon, out of patience, ordered all to leave him.

Alone he stood in the great hall, his mind in turmoil.

Then his son, Haemon, rushed in. He had heard the news and had come to plead with his father before it was too late. At first, he tried to humour Creon, but soon he saw that reasoned argument would have no effect. So he cried, 'Father, if you kill Antigone you must kill me too. I love her, and I cannot be parted from her.'

'You fool,' exclaimed Creon. 'You are talking nonsense!'

'But I love her, Father, I love her,' Haemon repeated. 'And as for what she did—I cannot find it wrong.'

'My son,' said Creon solemnly, 'you are young, and there are many things that you do not understand. When you follow me as king, you will find that the city must come first: the city, and its welfare and its laws must come before all personal desires. The king must uphold the law.'

'But this law of yours is not justice, it is despotism,' replied his son.

'If you insist in being so obstinate,' said Creon, 'leave me, do not waste any more of my time.'

The young count was silent, gazing at his father. Father and son were now so far from understanding one another that they might have been strangers standing there.

At last Haemon flushed angrily and said, 'Your friends may tolerate your madness. I cannot endure it. You'll see my face no more.'

'Get out,' spluttered Creon, 'get out, you insolent fool.'

As soon as he was alone Creon called his men at arms and ordered them to carry out sentence on Antigone. 'Take her away at once, and wall her up in the hillside cave as I have decreed.'

So Antigone was taken through the by-ways of the city on the way to her living death—and those who saw her could not keep back their tears.

Soon the king had another visitor. Led by a young lad, and followed by the members of the council, came the blind prophet Teiresias.

'What is this?' said Creon. 'Why are *you* here, Teiresias?'

'I will explain and you will do well to listen,' answered the seer, 'for you tread the razor's edge.'

Then Teiresias said that he had come to help Creon, who stood in great peril since his deeds had angered the gods.

But Creon mocked the blind prophet and insulted him. With dignity the old man reproached the king for his violent words and lack of understanding. Then, feeling for his young companion's shoulder, he said, 'Boy, lead me home again.' At the door he paused and raised his hand. 'I tell you this, King Creon, you will not live many hours before you give one of your own children to make amends for murder. Hatred for you is growing among the enemies of Thebes because of their dishonoured dead outside the city walls. You shall not escape the Fates, the avengers of the gods.'

When Teiresias had gone the members of the council urgently approached Creon. The leader said, 'My lord, the blind seer has left us with a threat of doom. There is not one prophecy that he has made against Thebes in the past which has not been fulfilled. This is no time for wrong decisions.'

'I know it,' said Creon. 'To yield is very hard, but I am terrified. What shall I do? Advise me, I will listen.'

'Release Princess Antigone without delay,' the oldest councillor answered. 'And lay the unburied body of her brother properly in its tomb. Act at once, for the destroying hand of heaven is quick to punish human error.'

After a moment's thought Creon said, 'I give way.'

'Go then quickly,' they all said, 'do it yourself and do not leave it to others.'

So Creon called aloud to the guards. 'Away at once up to the hills, take your implements and set free the Princess Antigone.' Then he ordered others to fetch the body of Polyneices—and to give it holy washing before committing it to the funeral fire.

Creon, accompanied by some soldiers, set out for Antigone's cavern prison. They climbed up and up, and coming near the cave heard Haemon's voice raised in bitter lamentation. Creon groaned aloud in anguish—'That is my son's voice,' he said. 'Hurry, men, race on ahead of me to the cave and find out if Haemon is in truth there.' It was too late.

Antigone was dead. At the far end of the cave she hung from a rope made from her garments. Count Haemon embraced her lifeless body, loudly lamenting her loss and cursing his father. Creon sprang towards him. 'What is this madness?' he cried. 'Come out, my son, my son, come out I implore you.' Anger blazed in Haemon's eyes. He glared at his father and spat in his face. Then he drew his doublehilted sword, turned it against himself and drove it halfway through his body. He cast the weapon aside and with his last strength clasped the body of Antigone, his life-blood staining her gown, and so died.

Then bitterly did Creon repent of his arrogance and pride. Gathering the body of his son into his arms he slowly made his way down the hillside.

As the mournful group re-entered the palace, a messenger ran to Creon, 'My lord, you clasp a burden of sorrow in your arms. Now within your house a second tragedy awaits you. The queen, true mother of her son, is dead. In grief she drove a blade within her heart.'

Creon prayed for death, but the wise old leader of his council said, 'Pray no more; from suffering that has been decreed no man will ever find escape.' Then King Creon cried, 'My rash blindness has killed both my wife and son. Friends, take me away, far from the sight of men—on me has fallen a doom greater than I can bear.'

Thus was the sin of Laius expiated by his family, and his line was no more. And thus was the despotism of Creon punished, and the prophecy of the blind Teiresias fulfilled.

True it is that of happiness, far the greatest part
Is wisdom, and reverence towards the gods.
Proud words of the arrogant man, in the end
Meet punishment, great as his pride was great . . .
Till at last he is schooled in wisdom.

Baucis and Philemon

Of all the sins committed by mortal man, selfishness, greed and inhumanity were perhaps most quick to rouse great Zeus to anger. Those who, with wealth to share, shut their doors upon the stranger and hardened their hearts against the needy could expect no mercy from the lord of heaven and earth. There is a hillside in Phrygia which still, they say, bears witness to the time that Zeus himself came to earth, to punish the wicked and reward the good.

On this hill two trees grow side by side, their leaves touching whenever the wind moves the boughs. A low wall seems to enclose them, perhaps the remains of a noble building; beyond are stretches of shining marshland waters, fringed with rushes, the haunt of coot and cormorant and other fenland birds.

Long ago this marsh had been a crowded, prosperous town of wealthy citizens whose lives were free from care. But comfort and riches had made the people not generous but evil, mean and grudging to gods and men; they had little thought beyond their own pleasures. News of the city rose to high Olympus, and Zeus decided to probe the report himself, and not through some envoy or messenger; he did, however, call his son Hermes to accompany him. Appearing in the guise of travellers, the two gods came to that city.

Rumour, they found, was all too true; the town was no place for homeless man or beast. They went from house to house, careful not to omit a single one. But the richer the smells of roasting meat from within, the more certain they were of curses and slammed doors. From a thousand housewives, they had not a crust of bread, not a cup of water, nor the use of a bench to rest themselves for an hour.

At last, only one place remained to try, somewhat apart from the rest, on the lower slopes of the hills. This was a solitary cottage, thatched with reeds—so small, indeed, that it was hardly more than a hut. But it had sheltered an old couple, Philemon and Baucis, ever since their marriage long ago. And though in a lifetime they had gained almost nothing in worldly possessions, few could match them in happiness and

content. Their one companion was a goose, which served as watch-dog in that lonely place. Roused by the bird, they looked out, and saw two weary travellers trudging up the slope towards their home. 'Ah, poor souls,' said Baucis, 'we know what kind of a greeting our neighbours below must have given them. And the next town is many leagues away.' Stepping forward with welcoming hands, husband and wife invited the pair to rest and eat before the next stage of their journey.

And so Zeus and Hermes entered, through a doorway so low that they had to bend their godly heads. But once they were in the cottage, nothing was spared to comfort them, not as gods but as tired wayfarers. First, Philemon set out two chairs—the place possessed no more—while Baucis busily covered the roughness of the wood with pieces of coarsely woven cloth. Then, while the old man went outside to gather herbs and vegetables from their garden patch, she bent down to stir and fan the half-warm ashes in the hearth, tempting them with dry leaves and strips of bark until they burst into cheerful flames. These she fed with dried twigs and finely split sticks kept hanging in bundles overhead, and when the fire roared merrily, she placed her cooking pot over the heat. Into this pot went a cabbage stripped of its outer leaves, and other of Philemon's herbs and vegetables. While these simmered, the old man took a two-pronged fork and lifted down a side of well-smoked bacon from the blackened rafters. From this precious store a piece was cut and added to the bubbling stew. Then Baucis took the beechwood bowl, which hung on a nail by its curved handle, filled it with warm water, and placed it, with a clean towel, for the guests so that they might refresh themselves and wash the dust of the roads away. Every now and then either Baucis or her husband would pause in their work to make pleasant conversation, telling the history of this or that, asking what the travellers had seen on their way, so that they should feel welcome and at ease, and not notice the long wait for food.

But, at last, the meal was ready. Philemon pulled out a bench of willow wood, and over it placed a narrow cushion stuffed with reeds and grass. This was covered again with a special woven cloth. It was old and cheap to a worldly eye, but it was the best they owned, and was kept only for sacred holidays and other great occasions. This bench was for the guests, and the table was drawn before it. One table leg was shorter than the rest, but Baucis placed a tile underneath and made it steady enough. Then she wiped over the well-washed surface with sprigs of fresh mint, and set out the first course. There were wild cherries picked in the autumn and preserved in the lees of wine, there were endives, radishes, cheese, and eggs which had been lightly roasted in warm ashes—all in earthenware dishes. The jug that held the home-made wine was of earthenware too, with nothing to mark it out from any other such vessel but a raised surface pattern; to drink this wine (somewhat thin and sharp) the guests were given beechwood cups, wax-lined. Then came the hot stew from the hearth, and the wine cups were filled again. For dessert, nuts and fruits—figs and dates, apples and plums— were put in shallow woven baskets; also black grapes from the vine on the southern wall, and a golden honeycomb. The travellers sampled all of these with delight. 'I doubt if there are any sweeter fruits in all Olympus,' said the older one. 'And this wine, that lightens the heart—another cup, if you will grant me; and another for my friend: his cup, I see, is empty too.'

Another? the jug held scarcely enough to fill four of the beechwood mugs. The old woman put out a doubtful hand to pour out the last few drops—but she was amazed that the vessel was heavy, and brimming to the top. She refilled the beakers, and still the jug held as much as when she had begun. When the cups were filled yet again and the wine still reached the top of the flagon, she was overcome with awe and terror. Husband and wife looked at each other, then, fearfully, at their guests, whose faces now seemed half-hidden in the shadows. This renewing of the wine, which both had seen, was a miracle. They were surely in the presence of gods.

They knelt before the travellers and stretched out their hands in supplication. Would their divine guests forgive them for so simple a meal, such lack of ceremony? But how (both silently thought) could such poor folk as themselves offer a suitable feast or sacrifice? They gazed about the room, looking in vain for some object of value, and then, at the same moment they remembered their goose, and went to fetch it. But the sage creature had no wish to change its useful life for death, however glorious, in appeasing the gods. The old couple chased it till they were out of breath and exhausted, but the goose eluded every attempt at capture. Then it ran indoors and boldly went to the divine travellers for shelter.

'This wise and excellent bird must not be killed,' said the older visitor, 'there is no need for you to propitiate the gods. It is true; we are indeed Immortals from Olympus. But when heaven itself is darkened by news of human evil and greed, it is time for the gods to descend. I, myself, came to earth to test the charity of your neighbours. Alas the truth was as dark as all report. The gods work swiftly when they must, and even now the wicked are punished and the land is being washed clean of their iniquity. Come with us now; you will see what you will see.'

The strangers rose to their feet, the one tall and sombre, the other quick and light, and the old couple followed them, leaning on their sticks. Very soon they lagged on the steep upward track; but when Hermes turned with a secret smile and held out his hand towards them, they seemed to skim the ground as if their feet were winged. They were hardly a bowshot away from the mountain peak when Zeus stopped and spoke. 'Enough, good Baucis, good Philemon; now look back, and you will understand our haste.'

They turned and looked downwards. The town where no one would share his plenty had vanished entirely; in its place was a shining stretch of water, beautiful in the evening light. Only one dwelling place remained—their own, on the mountainside. And even as they watched, its cramped and narrow walls dissolved, rose up—their home was a gleaming temple. The thatch seemed golden, smooth; it was truly a roof of gold. The wooden supports were dazzling marble pillars; the low doorway had turned into tall carved portals. These were wide open, and the old people could clearly see that a patterned marble floor replaced the bare earth they had known. They felt a great awe; this must be the work of Zeus himself. But they wept for the townsfolk, drowned in the waters of the lake.

Zeus looked kindly at them. 'No cause for tears, my friends,' he said. 'If those worthless neighbours of yours lie dead beneath the water, well—those who do not give have all the more to lose. Whoever lets imagination die is already dead;

whoever takes for his family and himself from the toil of others, and gives nothing back of his own free will, is no more than a walking body, overloading the earth. But, as my son is reminding me,' he continued, 'whoever has imagination can always sup with a god. For remember, the eye of justice also sees the selfless and the good. You two, my gentle hosts, rich in imagination if in nothing else, have earned a fair reward no less than the rabble there below. Whatever gift you ask is yours. Think now and choose.'

Philemon and Baucis looked at each other; hardly a word or two passed between them, for each read the other's mind. Philemon spoke. 'We see this radiant temple as a shrine to Zeus, but it also has as its heart the home of our youth and age. We ask if we may return, living in peace as we did before, but serving also as guardians of the holy place. And since our lives have been spent together in such pleasant harmony, we also ask not to be parted in death; let us both quit the earth at the same time, that one may not have to bury and mourn the other.'

These wishes pleased the god, accustomed to hearing larger requests. And so Philemon and Baucis returned to their hillside home, now a temple of rare beauty, mirrored each day in the waters below, as were the reeds and birds; for many years they were its keepers and priests. Then a day came when Zeus looked down and saw them standing before the steps, wasted and bowed with the weight of years, though clear in mind; one was saying to the other: 'You remember when . . .?', each recalling some bright hour in their days.

When a god fulfils his promises he does so handsomely, and Zeus gave them not death but a new life together. Where old Philemon had stood was a noble, spreading oak; in Baucis's place was a lovely and graceful lime, greenest of trees. The trees outlasted the shrine itself, though the low wall still remains. Peasants who knew the pair have vouched for the truth of the tale; some add that a certain goose and a clay wine-flagon, which many declared they had seen in the old folks' living-place in the temple, had vanished at the same time as their owners. Pilgrims have journeyed far to gaze at the trees, those proofs of human goodness and godly recompense: indeed, few travellers ever pass without hanging a wreath on the boughs. The hero Lelex of Troezen, who told this tale to Theseus and his friends, said that he himself had seen the trees and had hung fresh wreaths of his own. 'For,' he added, 'those who have earned the love of the gods are as gods themselves, and are no less worthy of honour.'

Peleus and Thetis

When Zeus gave the realm of the seas and oceans to his brother Poseidon, Nereus, the wise and ancient sea god, retired to his kingdom in the great silent depths of the ocean's floor near to the shores of Greece. Here he ruled in peace, cared for by his fifty daughters, the Nereids. They were of more than earthly beauty, and the fairest of all was the youngest, whose name was Thetis.

Nereus, like all the sea-people, was immortal, and he had also the power of foreseeing the future. Having lived hundreds of years, and possessing this gift of prophecy, he had grown exceedingly wise, and the gods themselves often sought counsel of him.

It happened one day that the god Poseidon came from his own sea-palace to the halls of Nereus, wishing to talk with the old Sea-King, and found him feasting in royal state, sitting on a crystal throne and attended by the fifty princesses. The ancient king rose up to greet Poseidon, and placed him in the seat of honour at his right hand, and the beautiful Thetis hastened to bring him food and wine.

When they had well drunk and eaten, the sisters of Thetis began to dance, and as they danced they sang; their dance looked like the twisting and untwisting of coloured ribbons, for their flowing robes were in all the colours of the rainbow. Thetis, dressed in white, sat on a silver footstool at her father's feet. This was her birthday, and her sisters danced and sang in her honour. Poseidon could not take his eyes from the youngest sea-princess, and he said to himself, 'There is none her equal in beauty, not even among the goddesses of Olympus.'

The dance ended, and Nereus placed a chaplet of fifty pearls on the head of Thetis, saying, 'Each of my daughters, O Poseidon, receives such a coronet when she attains womanhood, and today I crown my youngest and fairest child. No mortal princess had ever so rich a dower, for every pearl is worth a king's ransom.'

'Most wise Nereus,' answered Poseidon, 'you and I know well that all the riches on earth are poor compared to the hidden treasures of the sea. Yet I will make bold to say that even the most covetous of men would rather wed this maiden than possess her crown of pearls.'

'Boldly spoken, indeed,' said the Sea-King, and he turned towards Poseidon with a smile. 'But enough of this. Tell me now what you desire, if, as I think, you come to seek my advice.'

'To tell you what I now desire,' said Poseidon, 'I must speak more boldly still.'

'Do so, my guest,' answered Nereus.

'I would wed Thetis,' said the god, looking down upon her with his keen blue eyes. 'I did come hither, Nereus, to seek counsel, as I have often come before, but I have seen a sight that makes me forget all else. And I ask for the hand of your daughter Thetis in marriage.'

'And should you not first ask,' said the ancient king, 'my advice on such a marriage? What if it be destined to bring ill-fortune?'

But Poseidon answered, 'Nay, I will hear no prophecy. Give me my desire, and let come what may.'

'Shall I give my child,' said Nereus, 'to one so headstrong, who will no more heed a warning than the waves whose lord he is?'

At these words, Poseidon's eyes sparkled with anger, and he rose up, drawing himself to his full height. 'Beware how you refuse me,' he cried, 'or you shall learn that I am lord not only of the waves but of all that lies below them. Yes, for when Zeus, my brother, took the throne of heaven, he kept for himself the realms of sky and earth, but to me he gave dominion over the world of waters. Mine are the seas and rivers, and all that is therein.'

'It is even as you say,' answered Nereus calmly, 'and we, the ancient people of the sea, must own you for overlord. But think not, Poseidon, that you can make us afraid. You and your brother gods, mighty though you may be, are not the first world-rulers we have seen, nor the last we shall see. Yet if, in a year and a day, your heart is still set on marriage with my child, then come hither, and you shall have her.'

Proud Poseidon's heart was touched by this gentle answer, and his angry mood passed away as suddenly as it came. 'Farewell then, old King,' he said, 'and farewell maidens all, until I come again. Sweetly have you sung in praise of Thetis, but sweeter yet will your voices sound in joyful bridal-song.'

So saying, he returned to his own palace.

Not long after this, it chanced that Poseidon visited his brother Zeus, in high Olympus. The gods, gathered at their banquet, began to debate: who was the fairest among the goddesses? Some said Hera, and some Athene, and some, Aphrodite, and others praised fair Artemis, but Poseidon kept silence. Then said Zeus, 'Brother, you alone have not spoken. For whom will you give your voice?'

'For none here,' answered Poseidon, 'and therefore I have held my peace. But if Thetis, daughter of Nereus, were to rise from the sea and come amongst you, your debate would quickly end. Neither in earth nor heaven is there beauty like hers.'

The goddesses heard these words with great disdain, and the gods smiled to hear the unknown sea-maiden preferred to the Queen of Heaven and the Queen of Love. But Zeus, more ready to believe his brother, asked where this lovely sea-maiden might be seen. Poseidon told him that the Sea-King's daughters came up on moonlight nights to play and dance upon the shore. 'If you would watch them unobserved,' he said, 'take the form of some bird, or one of the seals that sleep among the rocks.' Poseidon said nothing of his own love for Thetis, and he forgot that the heart of Zeus might also be moved to love by her beauty.

The very next moonlight night Zeus took the form of a sea-eagle, and perched upon a rock as though asleep, and while he watched Thetis dancing with her sisters, her loveliness cast a spell upon him, even as it had done upon Poseidon.

Zeus, the king of gods and men, sat musing and silent when the Immortals were gathered again round his table, until haughty, jealous Hera began to taunt him, asking him if he also had seen the sea-witch (for so she called Thetis), and been made dumb by her enchantments.

'I have seen the daughter of Nereus,' he answered, 'and little need, proud Queen, has she of witchcraft, for she is yet fairer than Poseidon told us. Neither the Evening Star nor the Morning Star is so beautiful.'

'Make her your queen, then,' cried the angry goddess. 'No longer will I be called the wife of Zeus, when he affronts me to my face. Oh, a glorious bride, truly, will you set in Hera's royal chair! Green eyes, has she not, and a fish's tail?'

Hera knew quite well that the sea-princesses had no tails (except the mermaids in the north, who belonged to a different family), but her wounded pride made her sarcastic and unwise. Now great was the astonishment and anger of Poseidon, when Zeus, instead of soothing Hera's jealous rage, answered sternly, 'As you say, wayward goddess! Bear witness, all of you, that Hera is my wife no more. Tomorrow shall see another queen in heaven, fairer, ay, and more gentle than this troubler of our peace.'

'Nay, O King,' cried Poseidon, 'this must not be. The daughter of Nereus is my promised bride.'

But when he told how Nereus had promised to give him Thetis, if he asked for her in a year and a day, Zeus smiled and said, 'My simple brother, the Ancient of the Sea, who sees the future, knew that you would not come back in a year and a day, because by then Thetis would have wed another. Do you not see how easily he beguiled you?'

'Bitterly shall he rue it, then,' said Poseidon, 'yet why should he deceive me? Besides, he said something of evil threatening from the marriage, and it comes into my mind that he would have given me his daughter with good will, but for that foreboding.'

'What evil might that be?' asked Zeus.

'I cared not to learn it,' answered Poseidon, 'for be it what it may, it shall not turn me from my purpose. Thetis is mine, I say, by her father's promise, and not even you, king of us all, shall take her from me.'

Zeus made no answer, but his brow grew black as the storm-cloud, and the light from his flashing eyes was more dreadful to behold than lightning. Poseidon did not flinch under that awful gaze, which no one else ever dared to meet. Even Hera sat overawed, and the rest watched the angry faces of the two great brothers in silent apprehension. All at once in the tense stillness a sound was heard without, and there glided into the hall a veiled figure, clad in white. Slowly she moved towards the throne of Zeus, threw back her veil and stood between the angry gods, stretching out a hand to each. Then all the Immortals rose up in reverence; Zeus himself took the newcomer by the hand, and seated her beside him on the throne.

'Too seldom, holy goddess, do you visit us,' he said. 'Welcome now and always, whatever be your errand. Have you seen a law broken or some injustice done in the cities of men, that you come to us, your countenance grave as if in sorrow?'

This he said because that goddess, whose name was Themis, was the guardian of justice in the world, and was honoured in every city. She was, moreover, a very ancient goddess, and had received from Earth, her mother, the gift of prophecy and the knowledge of hidden things.

She now looked calmly but sternly from one to other of the still frowning brother-gods. 'It is not men,' she said, 'who have caused my sorrow. This very moment the sky, O Zeus, has darkened at your anger, the sea, O Poseidon, has risen in tempest at your furious voice, and trembling mortals wonder for what impiety the gods are wroth with them. It is you, the gods, not mere mortals, who transgress the sacred laws of right and justice. Shall it be told on earth that the king of the gods put away his wife for her passionate words, and used his power to take the bride promised to his brother? Or shall it be sung among the noble deeds of Poseidon that he defied his brother, the king, whom he had sworn to obey? Cease this unhallowed strife, and turn your minds away from the daughter of Nereus, for were she ten times fairer than she is, you would not wed her, if you knew what would come of it.'

With downcast eyes and in silence those high gods listened to the rebuke of Themis. But when she rose up to depart they both prayed her to tell them what was that fate of which she spoke, promising that they would strive no more, but draw lots who should wed the sea-maiden, if they still desired her when they knew all.

'It is ordained,' said the wise goddess, 'that the son of Thetis shall be mightier than his father. That is the danger of which Nereus would have warned Poseidon. If one of the immortal gods marry her, her son could make himself lord of heaven and earth; for he would wield some weapon more terrible than Poseidon's earth-splitting trident or the thunderbolts of Zeus and his power would be irresistible. Easily would that new god overthrow you all.'

When Zeus and Poseidon heard this, they sadly took an oath to forget their desire for Thetis. Then said Zeus, 'What if some other immortal, perchance one of the Giants, our ancient foes, wed the sea-maiden, and rear a son to overthrow us?'

'Lest that should come to pass,' said Themis, 'let her be given in marriage to a mortal, then will her child be mortal also. Let the Sea-King's daughter share the lot of mortal woman, a mingling of joy and sorrow, and see, in his last fight, her son fall in battle.'

134

'Lady of good counsels,' said Zeus, 'tell us on whom shall we bestow such a bride.'

'There is a king's son called Peleus, a noble, upright youth,' answered the wise goddess, 'who dwelt of late in Iolcos, and is now in Thessaly with the wise Centaur, Chiron. You, O Zeus, think well of him, for you were his protector when he was in undeserved peril. Now, if it seems good to you, you may reward him as he deserves.'

'It pleases me well,' said Zeus. 'I have not forgotten that brave youth, who at the court of King Acastus was found guilty of a great offence on the lying accusation of the wicked queen. It was from the bitter sentence of death that I ordered Chiron to rescue him.'

'Then, O Zeus,' said Themis, 'will you not send Hermes with all speed to the Centaur's cave? Chiron, when he receives your orders, will teach Peleus how to win the sea-maiden, and will make all things ready for her marriage feast.'

Straightaway Hermes put on his shining winged sandals, and departed on his mission.

The song of birds was loud in the woods of Pelion as Hermes drew near to the Centaur's cave, and the ground he trod was carpeted with crocus and violets, and the scarlet wind-flower, for it was spring. Peleus and Chiron saw someone coming towards them through the sunny glade. Peleus thought it was a shepherd lad of the hills, for his eyes were holden, that he might not know the god, but the Centaur knew him, and said, 'Hail, friend! What may be your errand here?'

'It is for your ears alone,' said Hermes.

Then Peleus said: 'I will go in chase of roebuck or wild kid to feast your guest withal,' and he took his hunting weapons and departed. At evening he returned, bringing venison, but the stranger was gone; nor did Chiron speak of him: wherefore Peleus asked no questions, having learned the best of manners from the good Centaur.

Next morning Chiron said to him, 'Peleus, I need the juice of the yellow sea-poppy for a salve that I am making. Will you gather a handful of poppies for me?'

'Willingly,' said Peleus, 'only tell me where they grow.'

'On the sea-shore, not many leagues from here,' Chiron answered. 'But, to be of full virtue, they are best gathered by moonlight.'

'That is easily done,' said Peleus. 'The moon tonight will be almost full. At sunset I will go down to the sea and gather your poppies while the moon shines upon them.'

So Peleus went down the mountain slopes, and came upon the cliffs above the sea, and saw the waves break glimmering in the dusk below. There he sat and waited till the moon should give him light to find a path down to the beach. Then gradually the world was flooded with silver radiance, and through the warm still air the sound of clear voices singing came mingled with the murmur of the sea. Peleus sprang to his feet, and leapt down the rocks from ledge to ledge, drawn by the magic of that entrancing song. And then, as he reached the shore, he saw the singers, and stood spellbound with wonder and delight.

The daughters of Nereus were dancing on the level sands, covered only by their floating hair. Faster and faster flew their little feet, twinkling in the moonlight as if slippered with tinsel, and all the while their shrill sweet song rose up like the singing of a thousand larks. Then, unknowingly, the dancers came near him, as he stood in the shadow of the cliff, and the maiden who seemed to lead the dance, passing close beside him, turned her head and looked him in the face. Only for an instant he looked into her deep eyes, in colour like the violet shadows on a sunny sea, then, with a startled cry, she turned and fled into the waves. 'Away! away!' cried all the sisters, and, like a flock of white sea-birds, the whole company dived out of sight.

Peleus forgot about the yellow poppies; slowly and sadly he went back up the mountainside, and came to his cavern home in the grey dawn, and told the good Centaur what he had seen. 'O Chiron,' he said, 'unless out of your wisdom you can help me, I am a lost man from this hour. That song I heard is yet ringing in my ears, and the eyes of that sea-maiden who looked me in the face will give me no rest until I find her again. Tell me how I may win her, for the longing I have is like a sword in my heart.'

'Such pain,' said Chiron gently, 'must all endure, who, being mortal, look on immortal beauty face to face. Know, Peleus, that she of whom you speak is the youngest and fairest daughter of Nereus, the ancient Sea-King. Her father named her Thetis, which means "Spell-Maiden", because he knew she would cast a spell of longing upon gods and men. To win her I will tell you what you must do. Before moon-rise tonight hide yourself behind some rock upon the shore, and, when the sea-maidens come, watch until Thetis is so near you that you can seize her in your arms. Then hold her fast. But remember, the sea-people have many strange powers, so take care, whatever happens, hold fast, do not let her go, and say no word until first she speaks to you.'

Peleus did as Chiron bade him, and, when Thetis came near, he sprang out from his rock and threw his arms about her. At her sudden cry, all the other sisters dived and disappeared into the waves. Peleus felt Thetis tremble for a moment in his arms, and then she began to struggle with such violence that he marvelled at the power in her slender body.

Silently then they wrestled together in the moonlight, Peleus needing all his strength to hold the struggling maiden.

Then it seemed that Thetis vanished from his grasp. Peleus felt a searing pain and through his encircling arms ran a column of fire. Grimly he stood firm and despite his terror did not recoil. In a moment the fire became a stream of water, gushing with such force that it almost had solid form. Drenched by the cascade Peleus still stood fast and kept his arms as if he held the sea-maiden.

A cloud covered the moon, and suddenly Peleus felt a great weight in his arms, his hands clutching feathers, and powerful wings beating about his head and shoulders. He held a giant sea-bird, and when the cloud slid off the moon Peleus saw a savage beak darting towards his eyes. Desperately he shifted his

grip; with one hand he strove to encase the long-taloned claws, while with his other arm he tried to shield his head. Then, just when he felt his grasp must weaken, the horny feet became cold and soft and slimy. Quickly, using both hands, he fiercely tightened his hold, and saw to his horror that he clasped a slithering sea-serpent by the neck. Its shining black skin, ringed with green and purple, gleamed in the moonlight as it coiled and twisted, this way and that, in its efforts to free itself. With all his strength, his breath coming in panting gasps, he clung to the hideous creature, and would not let go. But now the soft mass turned muscular and firm, and his hands were embedded in the soft fur of a black panther. Although he was nearly spent his courage did not fail. The panther snarled and struck him in the side with its sharp claws, but still he grimly held fast.

And now, with the sea-waves at his feet, Peleus realised that the panther was changing. In a second it became an enormous slippery cuttle-fish which almost slid from his weakening hold. But Peleus held on as firmly as he could though sprayed from head to foot with stinging, evil-smelling liquid. Then, suddenly, the silent struggle was over. The silver-footed goddess, Thetis, stood before him in her own divine form.

'You have conquered me, Peleus,' she said. 'And I will be your bride.'

Now it was that Peleus, who had endured so much for love, wept with joy, and from exhaustion sank down upon the sand. Thetis knelt beside him and comforted him.

Peleus and Thetis stayed till daybreak in the shelter of the rocks within sound of the gentle lapping waves. She told him about her ancient race, and the powers they possessed, and that this was the first time a sea-princess had married a mortal. 'Great was your own endurance and your courage Peleus,' she said, 'but the gods of Olympus gave you strength, for they have willed our marriage.'

Then Peleus spoke of his love for her, and how he had seen her once, and would have died of grief if he had not won her. 'I will love you always, I will never leave you,' he said. Thetis smiled. She said, 'And I shall be your loving wife for just as long as you remember that I am a goddess, come to you from the sea. Never must you question what I do. Never raise your voice in anger. Never touch me roughly. The very instant you forget I shall leave you.' Peleus protested his love was so great that he never would offend her.

In the east the round ball of the sun showed above the earth's rim, gave colour to the dancing tips of the waves and golden streaks to the dark water. Peleus hung his cloak on the sea-princess's shoulders and said, 'Come now, and I will take you to the good Chiron, who has been to me a father.' As they left the beach Thetis stooped and gathered a handful of yellow poppies, saying, 'I will bring these to Chiron since it was through me that you forgot them.'

So Peleus and silver-footed Thetis went on together towards the Centaur's cave. As they walked, the goddess seeming barely to touch the ground, Peleus saw with wonder how every bird and beast would come to her when she called. Ringdoves and woodpeckers came fluttering round her, the baby rabbits scuttled to her feet, and even the busy squirrels hurried down from the tree-tops at her summons. And 'little brother' or 'little sister' she called them all.

In the late afternoon they came to the cave, and the Centaur met them upon the threshold. 'This is the Sea-King's daughter, O Chiron,' said Peleus, 'and she has brought you the yellow poppies.'

'That is well, my son,' said the Centaur, with his grave, kind smile, looking at the bruises and marks of conflict on Peleus, 'for I see that you have need of the salve which I am preparing.'

To the Sea-King's daughter he said, 'The Olympic gods are well pleased, O Thetis, that you should wed this youth. It is their wish to attend your marriage feast, and soon they will be here.'

Then Peleus and Thetis went in, and saw that Chiron had made ready a great feast, and they marvelled at his fore-knowledge. When the sun set behind the hills, dim shapes began to move rustling through the silent woods, and the lights of pine-torches twinkled in the forest's gloom. Peleus, whose tired body Chiron had bathed and anointed with the healing balm, came to the doorway, and looked forth into the gathering dusk. He saw the lights, which drew slowly nearer, and heard the sound of wild, sweet music.

And then he saw a troop of Fauns coming from the forest, with torches and with garlands, playing on pipes of reed, and dancing as they came; and the lovely Dryads, emerging from their trees. There came also, following the piping of the Fauns, every beast and bird of the night: owls with solemn eyes, and prowling foxes, and a wolf with her cubs, and a lion, that rolled at Peleus's feet like a great dog.

When all were gathered about the cavern-door, the full moon rose above the tree-tops. Then suddenly the air was filled with melody so divine that the Fauns played no more but threw down their pipes and listened with awe-struck faces.

Louder grew the music, as of harps and voices mingled, and now from the clear heaven above rolled a peal of thunder, and the ground trembled. A great voice cried aloud, 'We are come, O Chiron, to the marriage of the Sea-King's daughter with the noble youth Peleus.'

At that voice the Fauns and Dryads bowed themselves to the ground, and Peleus also. The Centaur answered from the threshold, 'Hail, Lords of heaven and earth and sea, enter this my dwelling, for all things are ready.' Lifting up his eyes, Peleus saw before him a throng of bright-robed heavenly forms. Led by Iris, servant and messenger of the Queen of Heaven, the immortal gods advanced in stately procession.

First came great Zeus himself with Hera, followed by the Muses, singing. Then majestic Poseidon with Amphitrite, and Athene and Demeter; Aphrodite and Ares and Apollo and Artemis; then Hermes with his mother Maia, and the rest of the whole company of the gods. Dionysus brought a gift of wine in a gold amphora which he carried on his back. Amongst the great assembly were also the Graces, or as some called them the Charities, whose presence was necessary to the marriage ceremony. Seldom, if ever, had the earth seen so glorious a spectacle, and this was to be the last time Zeus and the gods so honoured a mortal's marriage.

The great and lofty cavern-chamber was ablaze with torch-lights, and the heavenly guests were seated on twelve thrones in a half-circle at the upper end. In the highest place, between Zeus and Poseidon, sat Thetis the Sea-King's daughter, veiled with a veil of silvery sheen; it was woven out of gossamer and moonbeams by the forest spiders, who weave all the robes for the Dryads. Peleus was beside her, and all the Immortals gave him greeting. The celebrations now went forward with mirth and laughter and rejoicing, and the gods praised the feast Chiron had prepared. And Dionysus poured wine into tall golden goblets.

The good Centaur had made the forest guests welcome also at the lower end of the cavern and had provided such food as each liked best. Even the beasts and birds had their share of the banquet. When the feast was over, Apollo took up his lyre and played, while the violet-crowned Muses rose up and sang together. First they sang the praise of Zeus their Father, Lord of All, and next of the lovely bride, silver-footed Thetis, the pearl of the sea, whom the gods had bestowed on Peleus.

Then Apollo struck a deeper chord from his lyre, and sang thus of the days to come:

A wondrous child, the son of Peleus and Thetis, shall be reared in this cave by Chiron's fostering care. That child, even from six summers old, shall hurl his small javelin with true aim and godlike strength at bear and lion that prowl near the cavern's mouth. And Artemis, goddess of the chase, and valiant Athene will come many a time to watch unseen those feats of the little hunter. But when the boy, trained and taught by the wise Centaur in all noble ways, comes to the prime of his glorious youth, then, in the company of princely warriors, he shall cross the seas and do battle beneath the walls of a far city, and win himself an everlasting name. For, long after that city has fallen, the lips of a mortal minstrel, poor and blind, will sing the deeds of Achilles, the son of Thetis and Peleus, in such a deathless lay that his memory shall endure till the end of time.

The song ceased, and all who heard it sat awhile in silence, musing on that prophecy. Suddenly, while the last notes of song still echoed in the ears of the silent assembly, a figure appeared in the doorway. It was Eris, the goddess of Strife, whom Zeus had not invited to the marriage feast. Her eyes blazing with rage, she stood erect for a moment, and then with a cruel laugh she tossed a golden apple into the centre of the company, and cried, 'Here, O Zeus, is my present! It will destroy the harmony of this moment's pleasant scene; and will bring also grief and strife in years to come.' She looked defiantly into the angry eyes of the lord of the gods and with a scornful glance round the shocked circle of the Immortals, she turned and was gone.

The apple rested at the feet of Peleus, who slowly stooped and picked it up. Wonderingly he looked at it and

then with a flushed countenance he made a sign to Hermes to give it to Zeus. Still angry at Eris's presumption the great god turned the apple in his hand and then slowly read aloud the words inscribed around it: 'To the Fairest'. The tense company watched as, at these words, Hera, the Queen of Heaven, and Aphrodite and Athene, glaring at one another, each rose from her seat and claimed the apple. But Zeus raised his hand, and sternly spoke. 'This is no time for unseemly rivalry. Truly, as she said, Eris has brought disharmony to our festival, but we must not allow her to spoil the happiness of the occasion. And you, my beautiful Queen, and you, my no less beautiful companions, must obey me.'

Hera moved as though to speak, but Zeus gave her no chance to interrupt. He continued, 'This malicious gift, and the jealousy it has aroused, must now be put out of mind. But do not doubt that I shall later appoint a suitable judge to deal fairly with you in what is a delicate, troublesome and most vexatious matter.' Zeus then signed to Apollo to play, and with the sound of soft music the tension lessened. A sigh of relief rose from Thetis and Peleus, and from the assembled guests, and soon smiles replaced frowns as Hera, Aphrodite and Athene forgot, for a time, their anger and injured pride.

Under cover of the music Zeus gave the apple to Hermes, charging him, in low tones, to guard it well and secretly until such time as he received further orders. Then with jovial smile and in cheerful voice, he spoke aloud. 'The song that Apollo made is his wedding gift. Let us now declare what we have brought for Peleus and his bride.'

Glittering armour, fit for a god, all studded with gold and silver, and a crested helmet, were the gifts of the Immortals of Olympus to Peleus. And Chiron gave his pupil a spear, cut and shaped from an ash tree, which possessed a greater power than was apparent from its plain appearance. Poseidon presented Peleus with a pair of noble steeds to draw his chariot; these horses came from an immortal strain—and their names were Bayard and Piebald. To Thetis the goddesses gave golden chains and bracelets, a bejewelled girdle and flower sprays cunningly formed from sea-blue sapphires.

But now it was past midnight, and the torches began to burn low in the vaulted chamber; once more Apollo's lyre was heard. He played a stately marching measure, and all the immortal guests rose and passed in solemn majesty out of the cavern.

Peleus and Thetis followed them, but by the time they came out into the moonlight, the gods had already departed and were gone from their sight. Only the Fauns, with re-lighted torches, and the Dryads, their hands full of flowers, remained. Then Chiron said, 'Go now, my children, with those who will lead you to the home prepared for you.' And so, led by the forest people, to the sound of sweet wild pipings and laughter, Thetis and Peleus walked into the green heart of the woods, and came to a hunting-lodge built of unbarked fir logs, and thatched with reeds and moss. The door stood open, a wood-fire burned upon the hearth and Peleus led the Sea-King's daughter inside.

The Apple of Discord

When the Immortals from Olympus had come in majesty to attend the wedding of silver-footed Thetis, goddess of the sea, and Prince Peleus, the feast was interrupted by Eris, goddess of strife, who was angry because she had not been invited. She flung down among the assembly a golden apple on which were the words: 'To the Fairest'. Hera, Aphrodite and Athene began to quarrel, for each claimed it as her due. To restore harmony, Zeus took charge of the apple and said he would arrange for a judge to choose between the three goddesses.

Aphrodite, Athene and Hera, his wife, gave the Lord of Heaven no peace until he kept his promise, so at last Zeus summoned Hermes. 'Go to Mount Ida, near Troy,' he said, 'and seek out Paris, the young shepherd who pastures his flocks on the hillside meadows. He is the handsomest of mortal men, and is known for his impartiality. Take him the golden apple and command him to give it to the fairest of the three goddesses.' 'But, Lord Zeus, my Father,' answered Hermes, 'she to whom this youth awards the prize will be his friend, and the other two will for ever bear him ill-will.' 'Exactly so,' said Zeus, and he smiled. 'And that is why I choose a mortal to judge in this delicate matter. It is not seemly that Olympus should echo with the sounds of quarrelling. If I myself made the choice I should never be free from the sulky, injured pride and complaints of the two who were disappointed.'

The shepherd on Mount Ida was, although he himself did not know it, the youngest son of King Priam of Troy. Just before he was born his mother, Hecuba, dreamed a terrifying dream. She dreamt that instead of a child she gave birth to a flaming torch which set fire to the whole city. Priam sought an explanation from the priests and prophets and was told to destroy his new-born son, for if the baby were allowed to live, he would bring calamity to his family and ruin to the city. The king could not bring himself to kill the beautiful child, so he sent for Agelaus, his herdsman, and instructed him to do so. But Agelaus exposed the child on a rocky spot, believing that death should soon come. To his astonishment some days later the herdsman found that a she-bear had suckled the infant and cared for him. So he took the baby Paris home in his leather bag to be brought up with his own infant son. The child grew into a brave and handsome lad. The nymph Oenone fell in love with him and they married. Paris took pride in the herds under his charge, and, in particular, the champion white bull which he crowned with a laurel wreath after it had defeated the bulls of all other neighbouring herds. He then promised a crown of gold to any bull which was more handsome than his. Ares, to amuse himself and to test Paris, assumed the shape of a bull. Being a god, Ares was of course perfect, even when he took the form of a bull, and Paris awarded him the golden crown. This event had been observed in Olympus, and Zeus thought of Paris as an incorruptible judge.

Hermes sought out the young man on Mount Ida. Paris, recognising the glorious messenger of the gods, covered his eyes in fear and attempted to hide. But Hermes called him, handed him the golden apple and gave him Zeus' commands. Paris' hair stood on end with fright. 'Who am I, a humble herdsman, to choose between the divinities of Olympus? Terrible will be the revenge taken on me by the two goddesses who must needs be disappointed. And indeed why should they, or any of the Immortals, pay attention to my judgement?' Hermes told him that the three goddesses had agreed to accept his decision without argument. 'And now I will bring them to you,' he said. So in the sunlit glade on the mountainside, Hera, Athene and Aphrodite, gorgeously attired, came before

the young herdsman. In a flash of gold Hermes disappeared, leaving them with Paris.

Never had mortal man been in such a dilemma. Holding the golden apple in his hand, Paris, abashed, dropped his eyes as the three divinities approached. He heard a quiet, firm voice: 'Look up, young man. If you choose me I will give you power and your name will be famous.' Paris took courage, looked up and saw Queen Hera near him. It was she who had spoken. Great dignity was in her bearing and her face and form were of majestic, unearthly beauty. Then Athene came nearer. 'Choose me, and I will give you wisdom.' The warrior goddess, now in softly flowing robes, which served to accentuate her perfect limbs, was looking down at him with her calm grey eyes. Paris squared his shoulders. 'Power,' he said to himself. 'I might become ruler of the world. But then, wisdom and knowledge—would it not be better to be known for these qualities of mind?' While he thought in this way, his senses were assailed by a fragrance so intoxicating that his knees trembled and his heart beat fast. Aphrodite, goddess of love, stood before him. She murmured

in a low voice, 'Choose me, Paris, and I will give you, handsomest of mortal men, the most beautiful woman in the world for your wife.' Paris hesitated for the space of half a breath, and then, speechless, handed the apple to Aphrodite.

The goddess of love laughed, a low triumphant laugh, and turned from him. The sunshine left the glade, the three goddesses vanished. Paris was alone, and only the disappearance of the apple convinced him that what had happened was not a dream.

Soon after this men came up from Troy in search of a fine bull. They chose the white champion from the herd tended by Paris, and took it in the king's name. 'For what reason?' asked Paris. 'For a prize in the games held every year in honour of Priam's youngest son, who died in infancy,' they told him. 'Can anyone enter for the contests?' asked Paris. 'The games are open to all,' the men answered, 'but the sons of Priam are fine athletes and they take the prizes, year after year.' Paris decided to accompany his bull, and to compete in the games.

To the astonishment of all spectators, and the chagrin of the princes, it was Paris who was crowned the champion. The prophetess Cassandra looked at him keenly and told Priam that this was his youngest son of fateful destiny. After questioning Paris and the herdsman Agelaus the old king embraced the astonished youth, informed him of his parentage, and presented him to the people as their prince.

When the priests of Apollo reminded the king of Hecuba's dream and told him that Paris must be put to death, Priam answered, 'Better the city should fall than my wonderful son should die.'

Now that his life had become so changed, Paris forgot Oenone, the nymph on Mount Ida, who had loved him so dearly. And, as the Fates willed, and as Aphrodite directed, the newly-found prince got ready for a voyage to the court of Menelaus.

Thus were the seeds sown for the beginnings of the war that was to last for years, and cost the lives of great heroes and their armies. It is said that Zeus had planned this catastrophe. For the great Earth Mother groaned under the weight of men, whom she could no longer support. Zeus, Lord of Olympus, hearing her sighs, decided to lessen the number of mankind by a war of such magnitude that thousands would perish.

The Childhood of Achilles

Peleus, ruler of the Myrmidons and King of Phthia, and his goddess-wife, Thetis, the silver-footed daughter of the sea, lived in great happiness, which was crowned when Thetis gave birth to a child, a beautiful baby boy whom they named Achilles. But although Thetis rejoiced in her little son she was anxious about his future. Fate had foretold that he might choose between a long, happy but inglorious life, or great renown as a warrior but death in battle while still young. Instinctively Thetis knew which her son would choose. She determined to try by her divine powers to circumvent the prophecy.

So one night, when the moon shone and the stars were bright, Thetis rose from the side of her sleeping husband, took the child and went out. She made the perilous journey to the Underworld and came to the banks of the dreaded river Styx. Here she unwrapped the baby and, holding him with thumb and forefinger by the right heel, dipped him in the sacred river. The immersion in the waters of Styx made him safe for the next stage of her secret work, and it also gave him immunity from grave harm and deadly wounds. She forgot that the heel by which she held him had not been covered by the river's water.

When she returned home Thetis rubbed the infant all over with heavenly ointment, from the crown of his head to the soles of his feet, then blowing up the dying embers until they glowed she laid her little son in the fire. Scarcely had she done so when Peleus roughly pushed her aside and snatched up the baby. 'Thetis,' he cried, 'what in the name of the sacred gods are you doing? Are you mad?' Sadly Thetis answered, 'It is you who are mad, you foolish mortal! Two or three minutes more and our child would not have been subject to the common lot of man. He would have been immortal like the gods. Could you not trust me?' In vain Peleus tried to explain. He had wakened and found her gone. Their child was gone too, and he feared both had left him. Then he had seen Thetis laying the child on the fire, and he was terrified.

Thetis appeared not to hear his excuse. She embraced the child, murmuring that his good would be ever in her mind. Then looking at Peleus she said, 'I must leave you. You have broken your promise. You have forgotten my divine right; not to be questioned, never to be roughly spoken to or roughly handled. Farewell, husband, I return to my ancient home, the sea. Do your best for our son.' Then, lightly kissing him, she vanished.

Peleus sat all night nursing little Achilles in his arms. In the morning he was forced to think what he should do. There was no one he could trust with his infant son except Phoenix, who did not know all that was necessary for the full training of a young prince. Then Peleus thought of his old friend, Chiron, the king of the Centaurs, the one person who had never failed him.

As Peleus hoped, so indeed it turned out, for Chiron offered to undertake the upbringing and education of Achilles. Phoenix and Peleus went with the infant to the cave on Mount Pelion, and here Phoenix stayed on to care for the child.

They fed little Achilles on the marrow-bones of bears to give him courage, and on honeycomb to make him a speedy runner. The golden-haired boy grew up strong and bold. When he was only six he killed a boar which one night came snuffling round the entrance of Chiron's cave. Not long after that he brought back a live lion cub for his friends to see. He was so swift of foot that he could chase and kill the fastest stags, even when he ran barefoot after them. Artemis herself, the goddess of hunting, was amazed when she heard what the child could do.

Chiron gave the lad a thorough training in archery, hunting and in the use of spear and sword. Chiron also taught him rhetoric and music, and medicine too, for he was a skilled physician. The boy had a fine voice and often entertained Chiron's guests with songs while they enjoyed their evening meals. Achilles had a loved companion of his own age—his cousin Patroclus, whom his father brought on one of his frequent visits to the cave. Though neither as strong nor as gifted as Achilles he was a high-spirited lad and a devoted friend. He and Achilles soon became inseparable.

While Achilles was still only nine years old a great quarrel arose between the Greeks and the Trojans. Paris, prince of Troy, had, during the absence of her husband, Menelaus, king of Sparta, persuaded Helen, the most beautiful woman in the world, to elope with him.

In spite of the rage of Menelaus and his brother Agamemnon, High King of Mycenae, and their angry demands for her return the Trojans refused to give up Helen. So Agamemnon sent heralds to the kingdoms of which he was overlord, and also to the sworn allies of Menelaus, that an expedition was to be raised against Troy.

Although it would be a long time before the ships carrying warriors and army equipment were ready, Thetis was anxious for the safety of her son. Already there were speculations about the lad. Apollo's priest, Calchas, had foretold, to the astonishment of those who heard, that Troy would not fall without the help of Achilles—still a mere child!

Thetis visited her son and told him of the choice the Fates had offered; and as she had known, he did not hesitate, but chose the glory and short life of a warrior.

To save him for at least a year or two, Thetis suggested to Peleus that it would be wise to put Achilles in a safe and secret place, where the messengers of Agamemnon would not find him. So Peleus took his son and Patroclus to Scyros and gave them into the care of King Lycomedes, who kept

the lads in the women's quarters with his daughters and their companions. Although they were dressed as girls when visitors came to the palace—Achilles was called Pyrrha on these occasions—the youths, besides trials of athletics and dancing and playing with the girls, still kept up their training. They practised with sword and spear and bow; they raced and wrestled and went for long walks together exploring the island. They visited the tomb of the great Theseus, who had met his death on Scyros, and wondered whether they would match his exploits when they were older.

After years of preparation a great fleet was at last assembled at the port of Aulis, ready to cross the sea to Troy. All the mightiest kings and generals of Greece had joined the expedition, under the leadership of Agamemnon. Yet all, remembering Calchas's prophecy, were aware that Achilles, the wonderful youth, was not with them. No one had heard of him since he disappeared from Mount Pelion. It seemed as if he had vanished from the face of the earth.

At last it was agreed that Odysseus the Cunning should set out in search of him. Rumours led Odysseus to Scyros. Here, disguised as a pedlar, with fine linens and embroidered cloth and shawls; ear-rings, bracelets and other ornaments to sell, he was admitted to the apartments of the women and girls. Beneath the feminine finery he had concealed a sword, a small shield and a short spear. When he had almost finished his business with the king's daughters, and had noticed that one of the girls seemed attracted by the weapons, he gave a secret signal, and suddenly there came from outside shouting and a bugle-call to arms. Instantly the girl who had been handling the weapons threw off her robe and grasped the sword and the shield. Young Achilles could not contain himself when he thought danger was near, and so had been trapped into revealing his identity.

Odysseus now brought all the powers of his persuasiveness to induce Achilles to join the armies ready to lay siege to Troy. The young man responded eagerly and Peleus did not try any longer to restrain him. Before he left Scyros, Achilles married his loved playmate, the princess Deidameia; but although she wept, it was in vain that she tried to make him stay with her and forget war.

Then Peleus gave his son the splendid armour that had come from Zeus and also Chiron's great unbreakable ashwood spear and, for his war chariot, the two immortal horses, Bayard and Piebald.

Faithful Phoenix likewise prepared himself for war. He had loved Achilles from the cradle and would not leave him now.

With fifty ships, each holding fifty Myrmidons, Peleus' famous soldiers, Achilles and Patroclus set sail for Aulis, where the Greeks were assembled under the leadership of Agamemnon, ready at last to launch their attack on Troy.

Helen of Troy

Although she is always called Helen of Troy, Helen, or Helena, was born in Sparta, daughter of King Tyndareus and Queen Leda. She had twin brothers, the famous Castor and Polydeuces; they were inseparable during their lifetime and in death were not long divided, for Zeus set them as stars in the sky—the Gemini or Twins. She also had a sister, Clytemnestra, who married Agamemnon, king of Argos and Mycenae. Most people thought that Zeus was really the father of Helen, and that he had come to Leda, in the guise of a swan, when she was bathing in the river. Helen's beauty was such as to make this seem true, for she looked indeed a 'daughter of the gods, divinely tall and most divinely fair'.

Reports of her astonishing loveliness had spread beyond Sparta by the time she was ten years old. Theseus, king of Athens, visiting her father's court, fell in love with her when she was little more than a child. He seized her from the crowd during a festival, and rode away with her. But it was soon discovered that Helen was missing, and Castor and Polydeuces at once set off in pursuit. Following the road Theseus had taken they travelled fast and almost caught up with him. But they lost the trail so, collecting an armed escort, they rode on to Athens. Theseus was absent, and at first the citizens refused to admit that the stolen princess was in their country, but later, being fearful of the brothers, they told them that Helen was closely guarded at the little town of Aphidna, in the care of the king's mother. After a skirmish Castor and Polydeuces freed their sister and took Aithra, the mother of Theseus, as bond-woman to Helen.

Back in Sparta Helen grew to young womanhood, and her beauty was likened to that of the goddess Aphrodite. Suitors from the whole of Greece, all men of wealth and distinction, asked Tyndareus for her hand in marriage. Greatest among the kings and princes was Agamemnon, who pressed the suit of his brother Prince Menelaus; and among the chiefs and warriors were the valiant heroes Diomedes, Ajax, Antilochus the son of Nestor, and Philoctetes who had the arrows of Heracles.

King Tyndareus knew that he could not choose a husband for Helen from this great company of rivals without making enemies for his daughter and for Sparta. He sought the counsel of Odysseus for help in this delicate problem. Now Odysseus was in Sparta with the other kings and princes seemingly as a suitor for Helen but in truth he loved Penelope, niece of King Tyndareus. He was sure in his own mind that there was no likelihood of his being considered a suitable husband for the beautiful princess since his kingdom was small and he was neither wealthy nor handsome. He suggested a plan which Tyndareus at once saw was a way out of his difficulty. The king called an assembly of the suitors and announced that Helen would herself choose among them but only if they would agree to accept her decision, and swear an oath to give help in time of need to her husband, whosoever he might be. All bound themselves by the oath, and Helen chose Menelaus. He was the most wealthy of her suitors and he was also kind-hearted, a man of noble nature who bore himself like a king. Then in gratitude Tyndareus gave the wise and gracious Penelope to Odysseus for his bride.

Menelaus and Helen were married, and not long afterwards Menelaus inherited the throne of Sparta from his father-in-law. They had been married ten years and a daughter, Hermione, had been born to them when, on an ill-fated day, Prince Paris of Troy came to the Spartan court, sent by the goddess Aphrodite to fulfil her promise: that he, the most handsome of mortal men, should have the fairest woman in the world for his wife.

Helen soon became infatuated with Paris, who left her in no doubt as to his own feelings. He drank from the cup where her lips had touched it, whispered sweet words in her ear and looked at her with the eyes of love. All unsuspecting, Menelaus left them together when he was obliged to make a journey to Crete. On that same night Helen eloped with Paris, bringing with her not only her own jewels and possessions, and her bond-women, but also much gold and silver treasure, priceless ornaments and precious stones from the palace. They made their way to Paris' ship and set sail for Troy, Paris taking Helen home with him as his wife.

Their marriage feast was held amid rejoicing and great splendour. The Trojans delighted in Helen, none could resist the spell of her beauty; and Cassandra's prophecies of disaster went unheeded. Antenor, a far-seeing Elder of the city, boldly criticised Paris. 'The Prince has done an evil thing,' he said, 'and terrible will be the consequences. Unless Helen and all the treasure she has brought with her are returned to Menelaus, we and our city will be destroyed.'

But the Council of the Elders neither condemned Paris nor listened to the words of Antenor, for the sight of Helen had bemused their wits and impaired their judgement. Even King Priam said, 'I will never let her go.' So the king and the chiefs of Troy were proud, and answered Menelaus with a curt 'No' when he came in fury to demand the return of his wife.

Paris gave no thought to prophecies of disaster or to threats of war. The goddess had promised him Helen of Sparta for his wife: he felt no shame in taking her from Menelaus. So for a time Helen and Paris were happy, living in the luxury that only Troy could provide, careless of the future.

Much of the wealth of Priam's powerful kingdom came from trade, and in particular trade with the East, and from the tribute paid by ships passing through the straits with cargoes of gold, silver and Chinese jade; fine linen; oil, hemp, and much else. The cloth woven by the Trojan women was famous and the plain was renowned for its fine breed of horses. Priam's son, the mighty Hector, was so skilled at schooling these spirited animals that he became known as 'the tamer of horses'.

The city of Ilium, or Troy, was really a fortress on the great plain of Troy guarding the entrance to the Hellespont. The city was barely a quarter of a mile across and was enclosed by high walls of great thickness, with watch towers and massive gates. The ground inside rose in terraces up to the royal palace, or citadel, in the centre, which held also the Senate Chamber and the rich pavilions of Priam's sons. The city's topmost dome was the great temple of Athene. Priam had treaties of trade and friendship with all his neighbours; it was only from the sea that Troy could be attacked.

When news came of the gathering of the hosts under Agamemnon at Aulis the Trojans prepared for war. After many months the watchers saw the skyline crowded with ships. They were the first in the fleet of more than a thousand ships come from across the seas to make war on Troy.

When the Greeks disembarked, their troops darkened the plain, and the shore echoed with the sound of their footsteps, while, in a fearsome, gloomy splendour, their polished arms and brazen shields and helmets flashed as they moved.

Hector then commanded the great Scaean Gate to be opened. Out went the Trojan warriors, men and steeds and chariots, led by god-like Hector, to oppose the advancing enemy.

There was little fighting that day. Hector realised that Troy had not enough soldiers to repel the vast army which was come against them, and after a few skirmishes he withdrew inside the city walls. To the Greeks the mighty fortress must have looked impregnable. They set up their tents, each company gathered under its chief, encamped upon the plain, and settled down to besiege the city.

For nine long years the Greeks fought against Troy. There were many battles between the two armies, in which brave warriors perished, yet neither side gained mastery. The Greeks indeed prevailed in the field but Troy maintained its strong defences.

From Olympus great Zeus controlled the destinies of both Troy and the Greeks, and Apollo, obeying his father, held the balance between the two, although in his heart he loved the Trojans. Among the other Immortals some were for this side and some for that. Aphrodite and Ares supported Troy, while Athene and Hera favoured the Greeks, Hera being set upon the total destruction of the Trojans and their city.

The bitter years of war were years of boredom for the frivolous Helen. She had soon tired of Paris and now she despised him. She was jealous of the great love between Hector and his wife, Andromache, and the joy they shared in their little son. Yet being without such heart's caring for herself, the trivial deprivations of war irked her. Since the Greeks now held the seaport none of the luxuries she craved could be had. Food and other supplies, the necessities of war, and friendly chiefs with their companies of fighters came overland and into Troy through the postern gates at the back of the citadel. But of this she took small count. She envied the daily excitement and danger of the women who went with an armed guard to the well outside the walls within sight of the enemy. And often, as she looked for them day after day, she wondered why her brothers had not come to rescue her, for she did not know that they slept their last sleep far away in her dear fatherland. It was only when she walked on the walls of Troy that she felt once more her power over men: when she appeared the fury of the fighting increased as both Greeks and Trojans were inflamed at the sight of her beauty.

By the tenth year of the siege Helen's heart was full of bitterness and despair. She felt herself a prisoner in the fortress city.

After a few indecisive battles the Trojans were granted an unexpected rest. The Greek forces appeared stricken by some plague or sickness that attacked both animals and men. The smoke of funeral pyres drifted across the plain day after day, and with the smoke came cries of mourning. It seemed no company was spared, for none came to attack the walls of Troy.

Then the sounds of mourning ceased and smoke no longer rose from the burnings. There was much activity in the camp of the Greeks and soon they came forth in battle array, advancing in a great cloud of dust, so close was their formation and so resolutely did they march across the plain. Hector ordered the gates of Troy to be opened and led out the eager Trojans. But before the armies could engage, Paris, clad in a panther skin, with a spear in either hand, came running from behind the Trojan lines, and called upon Menelaus to meet him in single combat. At this Menelaus leapt from his chariot and bore down upon the man who had stolen his wife and had caused the war. But when Paris saw the rage of Menelaus he was afraid and fled into the ranks of his comrades.

Then Hector turned back and caught hold of his brother. 'You are worth little as a fighter, Paris! How the Greeks will laugh and jeer at the champion of Troy! Your beauty of face and of figure, your fine head and curling hair, your harp—all will be of small account if you die a coward's death. But,' Hector continued, 'your challenge to Menelaus is an honourable means of ending the war. Therefore be a man; stand up to Helen's former lord. And we will make a covenant with the Greeks that whoever overcomes shall keep her.' And Paris said, 'Your rebuke is just, and I will fight with Menelaus for possession of Helen. But though you are a man of war, Hector, and have a heart of iron, love and beauty are also gifts of the gods, and not to be despised. Now, let us go forward to make a covenant with the Greeks if their commanders will agree.'

So Hector went out between the armies, and held his spear by the middle to keep back the troops on either side. And Agamemnon saw him and bade his armies stay quiet and listen.

Hector stood in mid-field, and said, 'Hear! ye Greeks and Trojans! Thus speaks Paris: all shall lay down their spears and other arms, while he and Menelaus fight for fair Helen and all her wealth. And let him that is victor keep her, and the rest shall swear peace and friendship.' Then Menelaus stood out and said, 'We will fight together, and let him perish that is doomed to die.'

The chiefs of both sides swore an oath to abide by these terms and, to seal their covenant, they sacrificed and poured out libations to the gods with prayers. Then the heralds marked out a space for the fight between the two husbands of Helen, and the troops, having laid aside their arms, sat down in ranks on the ground to watch.

All this while Helen sat at the loom in her room weaving a great purple web of double breadth on which she had depicted many of the battles between the Greeks and the men of Troy. There Iris came to her in the guise of one of Priam's daughters and said, 'Come, dear sister, and see what marvellous thing has happened. The war is stayed, and ranks of Greeks and Trojans sit in peace upon the ground: for Paris and Menelaus are to fight in single combat, and you will be wife to whoever is victorious.' These words stirred a longing in Helen's heart for Menelaus and her own country, so she left her room and went up on the walls, to where Priam sat with those Elders who were too old to fight. And seeing her the old ones muttered, 'Small wonder men should suffer for such a woman; she is in truth divinely fair. Yet better that she should depart from Troy before she brings a curse on us and on our children.'

But Priam called to her, and bade her come to watch the duel, and look on her old friends and kinsmen. 'I find no fault in you, dear daughter, for it is the gods who have brought this trouble to us all.' Then, pointing to warriors among the Greeks, he asked their names.

'That is Agamemnon,' she answered, 'the great king and overlord of the Greeks; he was my brother-in-law.' 'And who is that?' asked Priam. 'Less tall than Agamemnon but of broader build?' 'That is Odysseus, cleverer than most, and wiser; and there, head and shoulders above all the rest, is Ajax, the bulwark of the Greeks.' And so Helen named the chieftains, for she knew them all.

The combat was now about to begin. First Hector dropped

two marked pebbles into his helmet for the toss to settle who would first cast his spear. Turning his eyes aside Hector shook the helmet and it was the stone of Paris that leapt forth. Then Paris and Menelaus, bearing shield and spear, with swords hung at their shoulders, came to the appointed place.

The two warriors advanced toward each other with hate in their eyes. Paris threw his spear, striking the centre of Menelaus' shield but not piercing it, for the spear's point turned back. Then Menelaus, praying to Zeus that he might be avenged on the man who had wronged him, cast his long-shafted spear. It struck Paris, piercing shield, corselet and tunic, to graze the skin. But Paris was not wounded for he shrank back inside his armour. Then Menelaus, advancing quickly, aimed a mighty blow on the crest of Paris' helmet with his sword. The blow dazed Paris but caused him no harm for the sword broke into four pieces. Menelaus cried aloud in wrath to Zeus, 'I cast my spear in vain and now the sword breaks in my hand.'

And he rushed at Paris and caught him by the helmet and dragged him towards the Greek host, and would have taken Paris, for he was choking on the chin strap, had not the goddess Aphrodite loosened the band so that the helmet came off in the hands of Menelaus. He staggered and half fell, then tossed the helmet over his shoulder into the ranks of the Greek army, and with another spear charged forward. His enemy was there no longer. Unseen by any, Aphrodite had snatched up Paris in a cloud of mist and set him down in his own dwelling in Troy. Menelaus searched but no one knew where Paris was. Not a man in the Trojan ranks would have hidden him from kindness, for they hated him like death.

All had seen that Menelaus had overcome Paris, who was now no longer in the field, so Agamemnon arose in his place, and called out, 'Now, you sons of Troy, it is for you to give back fair Helen and all her wealth; then will we depart and leave you in peace.' Thus spoke Agamemnon, and the Greeks applauded.

So did the Trojans in the plain, and those who crowded the walls of Troy, for both armies desired an honourable end to the weary war. Happiest of all was Helen, now to be reunited with Menelaus, and to leave hateful Troy for ever. She drew the veil over her face to hide the tears of joy she could not hold back, and went down from the wall to her apartments. There lay Paris, among soft cushions, unharmed and unashamed. Helen greeted him with scorn. 'I wish that you had died by the sword of Menelaus,' she said. 'You boasted that you were the better man. Why did you not stay to finish the fight? Menelaus has been adjudged victor, since you were overcome and ran away.'

Paris explained that Aphrodite had taken him from the field. 'But,' said he, 'I shall fight with Menelaus another day, and slay him.' Then he spoke of love, but Helen turned from him and sought the company of her trusted slave, Aithra, who had comforted her since childhood. For joy had left her, and her heart was filled with dark foreboding: if the Immortals had saved Paris from death then it was not their will that the war should end.

Meanwhile the truce between Greeks and Trojans was maintained, and Agamemnon awaited his answer from King Priam.

The gods of Olympus sat in council in the hall of Zeus. Hebe had poured out nectar and they pledged each other in cups of gold, looking down on the city of Troy, Then Zeus spoke. 'Let us consider what shall next be done. Menelaus prevailed in the fight, for Aphrodite delivered Paris from certain death. Menelaus is without question the victor. Shall we stir up strife once more, or shall we let peace be concluded that Menelaus may take Helen to his home again, and Troy be left standing?'

And so he spoke, and all remained silent no matter what they thought, except Hera who could not contain her anger. Had all her toils, she demanded, to muster armies against Troy and crush Priam and his sons, been in vain? 'Tell me,' said Zeus, 'why you so pitilessly desire the downfall of this fair city of Troy. What evil have Priam and his sons committed against you? In truth, of all the cities of men that lie beneath the stars, I have loved holy Troy the best, where never have my altars been neglected nor my rites forgotten.'

Hera answered, 'Full well you know the reason why I hate the name of Trojan and the city of Priam. The stripling prince, this same Paris, did not award the apple to me—daughter of Cronus, and chief of all the goddesses of Olympus in that I am the wife of the King. Instead of exercising judgement he yielded to the common temptation of man. It is his folly that has caused this slaughter, and he shall not live to take pleasure in the wife he has stolen from Menelaus. He must perish, and his kindred and his city with him.' Then she smiled at Zeus and touched his hand. 'Are we agreed?' she said. 'If so, the other gods will not oppose us.'

Zeus said, 'Let there be no ill will between us over this. You shall have your way. But remember, if at some time I have mind to destroy a city that is dear to you, you shall not hinder me, since in this matter I have given in, although unwillingly.'

Hera answered, 'There are three cities on earth I love, yet if one or all of them displease you, raze them to the ground, I will not begrudge them to you. So send now a messenger to the Trojans and cause one of them to break the truce.'

Straightaway Zeus commanded Athene, 'Go down to the battlefield and contrive that a man of Troy shall break the truce.'

Swift as a falling star Athene went from Olympus, and taking upon herself the likeness of a high-minded Trojan, she came to Pandarus, the cunning archer, where he stood talking with his men. And the false Trojan tempted him, saying how all Troy would praise him if he killed Menelaus with an arrow from his bow. And so Pandarus strung his great bow, and while his comrades covered him with their shields, he took aim, and the arrow sped truly towards his quarry.

But Athene knew it was not the will of the gods that Menelaus should die. Instantly she was by his side and turned the arrow's flight so that it struck Menelaus where belt and corselet meet. The blood spurted for all to see, but the hurt was not grave. Then she returned to Olympus.

King Agamemnon saw the blood rush down over Menelaus' legs, from thigh to ankle, and ran to support his brother, fearing a mortal wound. Menelaus showed him that the barb of the arrow had not penetrated the flesh; a physician staunched the bleeding and put on a healing ointment. But King Agamemnon went in anger through his army calling on the men to resume the battle.

Among the Trojans there was shouting and turmoil as they hastened to arm and close their ranks in readiness for the onslaught. Like wolves the opposing armies charged each other. All day the battle lasted until the Trojans were driven back behind the walls of Troy. Then a brief truce was called that each side might collect their dead and succour their wounded. For Greek and Trojan soldiers lay in heaps upon the battlefield, so great had been the slaughter and so terrible the blows exchanged, on that day of broken faith.

In the fighting that followed the Greeks pressed hard upon the men of Troy, and seemed like to take the city. Then the Trojans offered all the treasure Helen had brought with her and much more besides (but Helen herself they would keep) if the Greeks would make peace. The Greek chieftains stood firm and bold: they refused to abandon Helen, certain that soon they would force the gates of Troy and enter the city.

During the destruction of Troy Helen was saved by Menelaus from those on both sides who desired her death, so great then was the hatred of that beauty which had cost many valiant lives and brought misery to Trojans and to Greeks. He took Helen to his ship, and with the rest of his fleet set sail for Sparta. Here both were welcomed by the people, and Helen, suffering neither blame nor criticism, was restored to her position of adored queen. Her only punishment was the gods' decree that she should bear no more children.

Helen and Menelaus did not die. When their time came they were together transported to the Islands of the Blest to live in perpetual peace and happiness under soft skies in a green and fruitful land.

Achilles and the Death of Hector

Agamemnon, overlord of the Greeks, called on all the princes
and the chiefs to avenge the wrong done to Menelaus, in that
his wife, the fair Helen, had been carried off to Troy. Thus
was a great host gathered together, even a hundred thousand
men and eleven hundred fourscore and six ships. At Aulis,
near Euboea, was their gathering, and from Aulis they crossed
over to Troy.

With Agamemnon, High King of Mycenae, and his brother,
Menelaus, King of Sparta, some of the chiefs of the host were:
Odysseus from far Ithaca; the noble warrior Diomedes from
Argos; Idomeneus, King of Crete; and from the Island of
Salamis the great Ajax with his brother Teucer, the archer.
There was also wise old Nestor, son of Neleus, who had
outlived three generations of mortal men, and, almost the last
to join the fleet of Aulis, the young Achilles, son of Prince
Peleus and Thetis the sea goddess. He came from Phthia, in
the north of Greece, at the head of his father's famous troops,
the Myrmidons, accompanied by old Phoenix and his dear
friend, Patroclus.

These, and many another hero, were with the ships that
came to the vast plain of Troy, which, watered by the rivers
Scamander and Simois, lay under the shadow of Mount Ida.
Here stood the city of Ilium, or Troy, tall and mighty, with
high walls, soaring watch towers, and, facing the sea, the
tremendous Scaean Gate.

For nine years did the Greeks besiege the city. They prevailed indeed in the field, but could not break through the
walls. Now, because they had been away from their homes for

so long a time, they were in want of many needful things. Therefore it was the custom to leave King Agamemnon with part of the army on watch, and with part to spoil the towns in the nearby countryside. And in this way the great quarrel that caused such trouble to the host came about.

The Greeks had sacked the city of Chryse, and part of the spoil awarded to King Agamemnon was the daughter of the priest of the temple of Apollo. For this dishonour to his priest Apollo came down from Olympus in wrath. Dreadful was the rattle of his arrows as he went, and his coming was as the night when it cometh over the sky. Then he shot the arrows of death, first on the dogs and mules, and then on the men; and soon all along the shore rolled the black smoke from the piles of wood on which they burnt the bodies of the dead. Then was Agamemnon persuaded to call an assembly of the chiefs to ask of the seer the reason for this plague of death; and the fault was Agamemnon's that he had not returned the maiden to her father, although the priest had come with gifts to ransom his daughter. And when the king knew that to stay the wrath of Apollo he must give up his prize, send her back to Chryse, with a hundred beasts for sacrifice, and claim no ransom for her, he stood up in fury and his eyes blazed like fire, and he demanded that the Greeks make recompense to him for his loss. And the share of the spoils of war he chose in recompense was the maid Briseis, who belonged to lion-hearted Achilles.

For this insult Achilles would have struck the king had not the goddess Athene, whom none but Achilles might see, restrained him, holding in her grasp the long locks of his yellow hair. Then Achilles vowed he would fight no more for Agamemnon in his dispute with the Trojans, and would only come to battle when Hector and the men of Troy threatened the ships that were his own and his own guard of Myrmidons. In anger he left the assembly. But King Agamemnon would not go back from his purpose. He sent his heralds to fetch the maiden Briseis, whom Achilles had won and whom he dearly loved. And she wept when she was led from his tent.

Now, the death rained on them by Apollo caused fear to stalk through the ranks of the army, and many there were who would go home, for despite the plague having ceased, they had no stomach for further combat. Among the chiefs also there were those who wished to take their men and ships and depart. But it was not the will of Fate nor yet of the gods, that the war should end thus, therefore Hera' and Athene inspired Agamemnon to instil throughout the host a willingness to return to the fight against Troy.

But the battle went against the Greeks, for Thetis had entreated Zeus on behalf of her son, Achilles, and Father Zeus allowed Hector, son of Priam, and mighty champion of the Trojans, to drive them back almost to their ships.

King Agamemnon could not sleep that night, for sore troubled was he in heart. From the Trojan city came the sound of flute and pipe, and the loud murmur of men's voices, and the light of many fires. He knew not what the enemy had in mind, and it seemed to him that he should seek the counsel of wise Nestor and the chiefs. So he arose, and drew his coat about his breast, and bound sandals on his feet, and wrapped a tawny lion's hide about him, took a spear in his hand and went out. He summoned Menelaus and Ajax and Odysseus and old Nestor, and other princes and chieftains. As they went through the camp they found all the watchmen awake and none sleeping.

They crossed the trench protecting the ships, and sat down in an open space, clear of the dead, even where Hector had turned back from slaying the Greeks. And Agamemnon said, 'We have need of good counsel that we may save the people. Truly the mind of Zeus is changed; for never hath a man wrought such destruction in one day as did Hector on the Greeks, yet he is not the son of either goddess or god.' And Nestor rose, and said, 'Is there now a man who will go among the sons of Troy, and see what they are minded to do?' Diomedes answered that he would go if Odysseus would go with him. He said, 'To have a companion gives comfort and courage, and indeed two wits are better than one.'

Then the two armed themselves, and both prayed to Athene that she would help them, and they went forth like two lions, stepping over dead bodies, and arms, and blood. Meanwhile, Hector had also sent out a spy from the city. This man the two saw, and they lay down among the dead till he had passed. Then Diomedes threw his spear to pass near him and stand quivering in the ground before him, and the two quickly laid hands upon him. And the man, Dolon, stayed still, trembling and pale, his teeth chattering with fear. And, because he hoped to save his life, he told them what they asked. No watch was kept, he said, save only among the Trojans themselves. The allies that had arrived that day, from the plains behind the city, slept secure, trusting in the Trojans' watch, and the last to come, the Thracians with Rhesus, their king, slept without guard outside the city, their magnificent horses with them. Then Odysseus and Diomedes slew Dolon that he might trouble the Greeks no more. And silently they went across the plain to where the men of Thrace lay sleeping. And twelve Diomedes killed and their king also, and Odysseus loosed the horses, first dragging the bodies clear lest the horses, unused to war, should jib at the sight and the smell of blood, and with his bow he drove them from the camp, for he thought not to take a whip from the chariots. And he whistled to Diomedes that he should come, and each mounted a horse, and, driving the rest before them, returned to the ships. Here their comrades rejoiced in their safe return, and praised them for all they had done.

And now Agamemnon caused a wall to be built and a ditch dug, which was both deep and wide, with stakes driven into the centre, to be a defence against the Trojans. And then, because Hector dared to be in the field and far from the city now that Achilles did not fight, the king was pressed by the chiefs to make peace with Achilles. So Ajax and Odysseus and old Phoenix were sent to plead with him, and to offer him rich gifts from Agamemnon, and one of his daughters in marriage.

When the ambassadors came to the tent of Achilles they

found him playing upon the harp and singing, delighting his soul with music, and Patroclus sat there silent waiting till Achilles should cease from his singing.

And Achilles jumped up, the gold harp in his hand, to receive his friends with joy, and they all sat down to wine and food. But when they began to reason with him and to entreat him to forget his anger, he would not be persuaded. He reminded them that he knew from his mother his own fate. 'I have no quarrel with the Trojans,' he said, 'for they have done no harm to me. Why must the Greeks make war against the sons of Troy? Was it not for the fair-haired Helen's sake? I fought for a woman I have not seen, and yet Agamemnon took Briseis from me, whom I loved.' And he refused the gifts offered by the king, and repeated that he would not fight till the Trojans came to his tent and threatened the safety of his own ships.

Then old Phoenix, weeping, spoke to Achilles reminding him of their long friendship. 'Child of my own I had not and thou wast to me as a son. I set thee on my knee and fed thee with choice morsels from the dish, and put the wine cup to thy lips. Many a tunic hast thou spoilt for me sputtering forth wine and food upon it,' he said; and he urged Achilles also to remember his father's warning to beware of pride of heart, yet still he refused to be swayed by argument. So Ajax and Odysseus departed, and carried Achilles' message to King Agamemnon. But Achilles kept Phoenix with him, and Patroclus prepared a couch for the old man.

When the next day dawned, Agamemnon called the Greeks to battle. Then the men of Troy and the Greeks leapt upon each other. As reapers reap in a rich man's field, making the barley and the wheat fall in long swathes, so did the Trojans and the Greeks slay one another.

But all the time Achilles sat in wrath beside his ships; he went not forth to fight but sat fretting in his heart, because he longed for the cry of battle. He and his Myrmidons stayed from the battle even when the men of Troy, led by Hector, pressing far from the gates of the city, advanced on the

Greek ships. So fierce was the attack that the brave Ajax was forced to give ground. And now indeed the men of Troy were at the ships; for Hector and Ajax were fighting for one of them. Ajax could not drive him back, and Hector could not burn the ship with fire. Then cried Ajax, 'O ye Greeks! Now must ye quit yourselves like men. For we are here in the plain of Troy, and the sea is close behind us, and we are far from our country. Wherefore our only hope is in battle.'

Then Patroclus, Achilles' dearest friend, ran to Achilles, and stood by him weeping bitterly.

Then said Achilles: 'What ails thee, Patroclus, that thou weepest like a girl-child?'

Patroclus said: 'Be not wroth with me, great Achilles, for indeed the Greeks are in grievous straits, and all their bravest are wounded, and still thou cherisheth thy wrath. Surely Peleus was not thy father, nor Thetis thy mother; but the rocks begat thee, and the sea brought thee forth. If thou goest not to the battle, fearing some warning from the gods, yet let me go, and thy Myrmidons with me. And let me put thy armour on me; so shall the Greeks have breathing-space from the war.'

So he spake, entreating, nor knew that for his own doom he entreated. And Achilles made reply:

'It is no warning that I heed, that I keep back from the war. But these men took from me my prize, which I won with my own hands. I said that I would not rise up till the battle should come nigh to my own ships. But thou mayest put my armour upon thee, and lead my Myrmidons to the fight. For in truth the men of Troy are gathered as a dark cloud about the ships, and the Greeks have scarce standing-ground between them and the sea. For they see not the gleam of my helmet. Go, therefore, Patroclus, and drive Hector from the ships. And then come thou back, nor fight any more with the Trojans. Go not near, in the delight of battle, to the walls of Troy, lest one of the gods meet thee to thy hurt; and, of a truth, the keen archer Apollo loves the Trojans well.'

Down at the ships Ajax could hold out no longer. For swords and javelins came thick upon him, and clattered on his helmet, and his shoulder was weary with the great shield which he held; and he breathed heavily and hard, and the great drops of sweat fell upon the ground. Then at last Hector came near and smote his spear with a great sword, so that the head fell off. Then was Ajax sore afraid, and gave way, and the men of Troy set torches to the ship's stem, and a great flame shot up to the sky. And Achilles saw it, and smote his thigh and spake:

'Haste thee, Patroclus, for I see the fire rising up from the ships. Put thou on the armour; and I will call my people to the war.'

So Patroclus put on the armour—corselet, and shield, and helmet—and bound upon his shoulder the silver-studded sword, and took a mighty spear in his hand. But the great Pelian spear he took not, for that no man but Achilles might wield. Then Automedon, the charioteer, yoked the horses to the chariot, Bayard and Piebald, and with them in the side harness, Pedasus; and they two were deathless steeds but he was mortal.

Then Achilles called his soldiers and said, 'Forget not, ye Myrmidons, the bold words that ye spake against the men of Troy during the days of my wrath, making complaint that I kept you from the battle against your will. Now, therefore, ·ye have that which you desired.'

So the Myrmidons went to the battle in close array, helmet to helmet and shield to shield, close as the stones with which a builder builds a wall. And in front went Patroclus, and Automedon in the chariot beside him. Then Achilles went to his tent and took a great cup from the chest, which Thetis his mother had given him. Now no man drank of that cup but he only, nor did he pour out of it libations to any of the gods, but only to Zeus. This cup Achilles first cleansed with sulphur, and then with water from the spring. And after this he washed his hands, and stood in the midst of the space before his tent, and poured out of it

175

to Zeus, saying, 'O Zeus, I send my comrade to this battle; make him strong and bold, and give him glory, and bring him home safe to the ships, and my people with him.'

So he prayed, and Father Zeus heard him, and part he granted and part he denied.

But now Patroclus with the Myrmidons had come to where the battle was raging about the ships, and when the men of Troy beheld him, they thought that Achilles had forgotten his wrath and was come forth to the war. Then the men of Troy turned to flee, and many chiefs of fame fell by the spears of the Greeks. So the battle rolled back to the trench, and in the trench many chariots of the Trojans were broken, but the horses of Achilles went across it at a stride, so nimble were they and strong. And the heart of Patroclus was set to slay Hector; but he could not overtake him, so swift were his horses. Then did Patroclus turn his chariot, and keep back those that fled, that they should not go to the city, and rushed hither and thither, still slaying as he went.

But then did Patroclus forget the word which Achilles had spoken to him, that he should not go near the city, for he pursued the men of Troy even to the wall. Thrice he mounted on the angle of the wall, and thrice Apollo himself drove him back, pushing his shining shield. But the fourth time the god said: 'Go thou back, Patroclus. It is not for thee to take the city of Troy; no, nor for Achilles, who is far better than thou art.'

So Patroclus went back, fearing the wrath of the archer god. But Apollo stirred up the spirit of Hector, that he should go against Patroclus. Therefore he went, with his brother Cebriones for driver of his chariot. When they came near, Patroclus cast a great stone which he had in his hand, and smote Cebriones on the forehead, crushing it in, so that he fell headlong from the chariot. And Patroclus mocked him, saying: 'How nimble is this man! How lightly he dives! What spoil he would take of oysters, diving from a ship, even in a stormy sea! Who would have thought that there were such skilful divers in Troy!'

Then again the battle waxed hot about the body of Cebriones, and this too, at the last, the Greeks drew unto themselves, and spoiled it of the arms. And this being accomplished, Patroclus rushed against the men of Troy. Thrice he rushed, and each time he slew nine chiefs of fame. But the fourth time Apollo stood behind him and struck him on the head and shoulders, so that his eyes were darkened. And the helmet fell from off his head, so that the horse-hair plumes were soiled with dust. Never before had it touched the ground, for it was the helmet of Achilles. And also the god brake the spear in his hand, and struck the shield from his arms, and loosed his corselet. All amazed Patroclus stood, and then he sought to flee to the ranks of his comrades. But Hector saw him, and thrust at him with his spear, smiting him in the groin, so that he fell. And when the Greeks saw him fall, they sent up a terrible cry.

Fierce was the fight about the body of Patroclus, and many heroes fell, both on this side and on that. Then did Hector strip off the arms of Patroclus, the arms which the great Achilles had given him to wear. But the horses of Achilles stood apart from the battle when they knew that Patroclus was dead, and wept. Nor could Automedon move them with the lash, nor with gentle words, nor with threats. They would not return to the ships, nor would they go into the battle; but as a pillar stands on the tomb of some dead man, so they stood, with their heads drooped to the ground, and with big tears dropping to the earth, and their long manes trailing in the dust.

Father Zeus beheld them, and pitied them, and said:

'It is not well that we gave you, immortal as ye are, to a mortal man; for of all things that move on earth, mortal man is the fullest of sorrow. But Hector shall not possess you. It is enough for him, yea, and too much, that he hath the arms of Achilles.'

Then did the horses move from their place, and obey their charioteer as before. Nor could Hector take them, though he desired them very much. And all the while the battle raged about the dead Patroclus. And at last Ajax said to Menelaus (now these two had borne themselves more bravely in the fight than all others):

'See if thou canst find Antilochus, Nestor's son, that he may carry the tidings to Achilles, how that Patroclus is dead.'

So Menelaus went and found Antilochus on the left of the battle and said to him: 'I have ill news for thee. Thou seest that the men of Troy have the victory today. And that Patroclus lies dead. Run, therefore, to Achilles, and tell him, if haply he may save the body; but as for the arms, Hector has them already.'

Sore dismayed was Antilochus to hear such tidings, and his eyes were filled with tears, and his voice was choked. Yet did he give heed to the words of Menelaus, and ran to tell Achilles of what had chanced. But Menelaus went back to Ajax, where he had left him by Patroclus, and said:

'Antilochus, indeed, bears the tidings to Achilles. Yet I doubt whether he will come, for all his wrath against Hector, seeing that he has no armour to cover him. Let us think, then, how we may best carry Patroclus away from the men of Troy.'

Then said Ajax, 'Do thou and Meriones run forward and raise the body in your arms, and I and the son of Oileus will keep off, meanwhile, the men of Troy.'

So Menelaus and Meriones ran forward and lifted up the body. And the Trojans ran forward with a great shout when they saw them, as dogs run barking before the hunters when they chase a wild boar; but when the beast turns to bay, then they flee this way and that. So did the men of Troy flee when Ajax the Greater and Ajax the Less turned to give battle. But still the Greeks gave way, and still the Trojans came on, and ever in the front were Hector, the son of Priam, and Aeneas, the son of Anchises.

But in the meantime Antilochus came near to Achilles, who, indeed, seeing that the Greeks fled and the men of Troy pursued, was already sore afraid. And he said, weeping as he spake:

'I bring ill news—Patroclus lies low. The Greeks fight for his body, but Hector has his arms.'

Then Achilles took up the dark dust of the plain in both hands, and poured it on his head, and lay at his length upon the ground, and tore his hair. And all the women wailed. And Antilochus sat weeping; but ever he held the hands of Achilles, lest he should slay himself in his great grief.

Then came Thetis, mother of Achilles, hearing his cry, from where she sat in the depths of the sea, and laid her hand on him and said:

'Why weepest thou, my son? Hide not the matter from me, but tell me.'

And Achilles answered: 'All that Zeus promised thee for me he hath fulfilled. But what profit have I, for my friend Patroclus is dead, and Hector has the arms which I gave him to wear. And as for me, I care not to live, except I can avenge him.'

Then said Thetis: 'Nay, my son, speak not thus. For when Hector dieth, thy doom also is near.'

And Achilles spake in great wrath: 'Would that I might die this hour, seeing that I could not help my friend, but am a burden on the earth—I, who am better in battle than all the Greeks besides. Cursed be the wrath that sets men to strive the one with the other, even as it set me to strive with King Agamemnon! But let the past be past. And as for my fate—let it come when it may, so that I first avenge myself on Hector. Wherefore, seek not to keep me back from the battle.'

Then Thetis said: 'Be it so; only thou canst not go without thy arms, which Hector hath. But tomorrow will I go to Hephaestus, that he may furnish thee anew.'

Yet while they talked the men of Troy pressed the Greeks more and more for the body of Patroclus. And, indeed, would have taken it had not Zeus sent word to Achilles: 'Rouse thee, son of Peleus, or Patroclus will be a prey for the dogs of Troy. Go to the trench and show thyself; so shall the men of Troy tremble and cease from the battle, and the Greeks shall have breathing-space.'

So he went, and Athene put the aegis of Zeus about his mighty shoulders, and a golden halo about his head, making it shine as a flame of fire, even as the watch-fires shine at night from some city that is besieged. Then went Achilles to the trench; with the battle he mingled not, heeding his mother's commands, but he shouted aloud, and his voice was as the sound of a trumpet. And when the men of Troy heard, they were stricken with fear, and the horses backed with the chariots, and the drivers were astonished when they saw the flaming fire above his head which Athene had kindled. Thrice across the trench the great Achilles shouted, and thrice the men of Troy fell back. And that hour there perished twelve chiefs of fame, wounded by their own spears or trampled by their own steeds, so great was the terror among the men of Troy.

Right gladly did the Greeks take Patroclus out of the press. Then they laid him on a bier, and carried him to the tent, Achilles walking with many tears by his side.

In the camp of the Greeks they mourned for Patroclus. And Achilles stood among his Myrmidons and said:

'Vain was the promise that I made to Menoetius that I would bring back his son with his portion of the spoils of Troy. But Zeus fulfils not the thoughts of man. For Patroclus lies dead, nor shall I return to the house of Peleus, my father, for I, too, must die in this land. But thee, O Patroclus, I will not bury till I bring hither the head and the arms of Hector, and twelve men of Troy to slay at thy funeral pile.'

So they washed the body of Patroclus and anointed it, putting ointment nine years old into the wounds, and laid it on a bed, and covered it with a linen cloth from the head to the feet, and laid a white robe over it. All night the Myrmidons mourned for Patroclus dead.

But Thetis went to the house of Hephaestus. She found him busy at his work, making twenty cauldrons with three feet, that were to stand about the house of the gods. Golden wheels had they beneath, that they might go of their own motion into the chambers of the gods, and of their own motion return.

Then did Thetis tell him of her son Achilles, and of the wrong that had been done to him, and of his wrath, and of how Patroclus was dead, and that the arms that he had had were lost.

'Make me now,' she said, 'for him a shield and a helmet, and greaves, and a corselet.'

And Hephaestus answered: 'Be of good cheer. Would that I could keep from him the doom of death as easily as I can make him such arms that a man will wonder when he looks upon them.'

Then he turned the bellows to the fire, and bade them work. Also he put bronze and tin and gold and silver into the fire, to melt them, and set the anvil, and took the hammer in one hand, and the tongs in the other.

First he made a shield, great and strong, and fastened thereto a belt of silver. On it he wrought the earth, and the sky, and the sea, and the sun, and the moon, and all the stars.

He wrought also two cities. In the one there was peace, and about the other there was war. And round about the shield he wrought the great river of ocean.

Besides the shield, he also made a corselet brighter than fire, and a great helmet with a ridge of gold for the crest, and greaves of tin. And when he had finished Hephaestus set them all before the mother of Achilles. Like a hawk did she leap from Olympus, carrying them to her son; him she found lying on the earth with his arms about the body of Patroclus, weeping aloud, and his men stood about lamenting.

The goddess stood in the midst, and clasped her son by the hand, and spake: 'Come, now, let us leave the dead man; for he hath been slain according to the ordering of the gods. And do thou receive from Hephaestus this armour, exceeding beautiful, such as man never yet wore upon his shoulders.'

So she spake, and cast the armour before Achilles. Loud did it rattle as it fell, and the Myrmidons feared to look upon the sight. But Achilles took the splendid armour into his hand, and was glad, and spake, saying: 'Mother, the gods have given me arms, such as it is fitting should be made in heaven, and I vow I will arm me for the fight. Yet much I fear that decay will mar the body of Patroclus, now that the life hath gone from out of it.'

But Thetis made answer: 'Let not this trouble thee; I will keep decay from his flesh, yea, though he should lie here till the year come round again. Go, then, and call the people to the assembly, and put away thy wrath against King Agamemnon, and arm thyself for the battle.'

So she spake, putting trust and valour into his soul; and into the nostrils of the dead man she poured ambrosia and ruddy nectar, that his flesh might be sweet.

Achilles then went along the shore of the sea, shouting aloud to call an assembly of the warriors. And at his call they came, even they who before had remained at the ships, such as the pilots, and they who dealt out the food, because Achilles, who had been absent so long from the battle, had returned thereto. Diomedes and Odysseus came to the assembly, leaning on spears, for their wounds were fresh, and King Agamemnon also came.

Then Achilles stood up and spake to Agamemnon: 'It is ill done, son of Atreus, that we quarrelled! Come, let the past be past. Here I make an end of my anger. Now make haste, let us turn without delay to the battle.'

Then spake the wise Odysseus: 'Achilles, urge not the Greeks to enter fasting into the battle: for verily the strife will not be short, seeing that both this host and that are inspired with might from heaven. A man that hath not eaten cannot fight all day till set of sun, for his limbs grow heavy unawares, and he is hindered by hunger and thirst.'

Then said the king: 'Thou speakest well, Odysseus. Do thou thyself fetch the gifts that I offer to Achilles to make full amends, and let a reconciliation feast be prepared. And let the herald fetch us a boar, that we may do sacrifice to Zeus and to the Sun.'

But Achilles said: 'This business had suited better some other time, as when there was some breathing-space in the war, and my heart was not so hot within me. But now the dead whom Hector slew lieth low, and ye bid me think of food. Let the Greeks enter fasting into battle, and make them a great supper when the sun goes down. As for me, neither food nor drink shall pass my lips.'

To him Odysseus made reply: 'Thou art the stronger, son of Peleus, yet I may be the wiser, for I am older than thou, and of more experience. Ask not the Greeks to fast because of the dead. Verily men fall every day. How, then, should there be any interval of grief? Rather let us bury him that dieth, and bewail him for a day, and harden our hearts to forget: and then let us who are left eat and drink, that we may fight with better heart.'

The chiefs would have Achilles feast with them; but he hearkened not, for he would neither eat nor drink till he had vengeance for the dead.

Then Zeus said to Athene: 'Carest thou not for Achilles that is so dear to thee? See, the other Greeks are gone to their meal, but he sits fasting.'

And Athene leapt down from heaven, and shed into the breast of Achilles nectar and ambrosia, that his knees should not fail from hunger.

Meanwhile the Greeks made ready for battle, and in the midst Achilles armed himself. He put the lordly greaves about his legs, and fitted the corselet on his breast. From his shoulders he hung the sword, and he took the great shield that Hephaestus had made, and it blazed as it were the sun in heaven. Also he put the helmet on his head, and the plumes waved all around. Then he made trial of the arms, and they fitted him well, and bare him up like wings. Last he drew from its case his father's spear, which Chiron cut on the top of Pelion, to be the death of many, and none might wield it but Achilles' self. Then he spake to his horses: 'Take heed, Bayard and Piebald, that ye save your master today, nor leave him dead on the field, as ye left Patroclus.'

Then Hera gave to the horse Bayard a voice, so that he spake: 'Surely we will save thee, great Achilles; yet for all that, doom is near to thee, nor are we the cause, but the gods and mastering Fate. Nor was it of us that Patroclus died, but Apollo slew him and gave the glory to Hector. So shalt thou, too, die by the hands of a god and of a mortal man.'

And Achilles said: 'What need to tell me of my doom? Right well I know it. Yet will I not cease till I have made the Trojans weary of battle.' Then he shouted to his Myrmidons and drove forward into battle, eager above all things to meet with Hector and to slay him.

Now Zeus had inspired the hearts of both the Greeks and the men of Troy to hurl themselves into battle. And as the combat waxed furiously there arose a dreadful strife among the gods by reason of the division between them (some being for one side and some for the other). With a great crash they came together so that the earth shook and the heavens rang as with a trumpet and Zeus heard the noise of their conflict from where he sat on high Olympus. Among those who supported the Greeks this day were Hera, Poseidon, Hermes and Athene; but Apollo and Artemis, the river god Xanthus, and Ares and Aphrodite helped the men of Troy.

In the midst of the battle Apollo snatched Hector from the sight of Achilles and bade him keep from the forefront of the battle. But many were the heroes that fell before Achilles, for he fought savagely and without mercy. And, although often impeded in his vengeance by the intervention of Apollo and other gods, yet sustained by Hera, Poseidon and Athene he ceased not to pursue and slay the men of Troy. So great was his onslaught that the forces of Troy parted before him, and wheeling he turned and drove them before him across the plain towards the city.

King Priam stood in a tower on the wall and sore troubled was he when he saw the progress of the battle. He hastened down to the guardians of the gates and said, 'Keep the wicket-gates open that the troops may enter in, for they fly before Achilles.' And the men hastened in, wearied with toil and thirst, and covered with dust, and they flocked into the city, nor did they stay to ask who was safe and who was dead, in such haste and fear did they flee. Only Hector remained outside the walls, standing in front of the Scaean Gate.

And Priam, from the wall, saw Achilles coming swift as a racehorse across the plain, his armour glittering bright as the brightest of the stars. And the old man groaned aloud, and cried to his son Hector, where he stood before the gates, eager to do battle with this dread warrior:

'Wait not for this man, dear son, wait not for him, lest thou die beneath his hand, for indeed he is the stronger. Of many brave sons has he already bereaved me. Come within the walls, dear child; come to save the sons and daughters of Troy; come in pity for me, thy father, for whom, in my old age, an evil fate is in store, to see sons slain with the sword, and daughters carried into captivity, and babes dashed upon the ground.'

Thus old Priam spake, but could not turn the heart of his

son. And from the walls on the other side of the gate his
mother called to him, weeping sore, and said:

'Come within the walls; wait not for this man, nor stand
in battle against him. If he slay thee, nor I, nor thy father,
nor thy wife, shall pay thee the last honours of the dead,
but far away, by the ships of the Greeks, the dogs and
vultures will devour thee.'

So father and mother besought their son, but all in vain.
Hector was still minded to abide the coming of Achilles.

And Achilles came near, brandishing over his right shoulder
the great Pelian spear, and the flash of his arms was as the
flame of fire, or as the rising sun. Then Hector trembled
when he saw him, nor dared to abide his coming. Fast he
fled from the gates, and fast Achilles pursued him, as a hawk,
fastest of all the birds of air, pursues a dove upon the
mountains. Past the watch tower they ran, past the wind-
blown fig tree, along the wagon-road which went about the
walls, and they came to the fair-flowing fountain where from
two springs rises the stream of eddying Scamander. Past the

springs they ran, one flying, the other pursuing; brave was he that fled, braver he that pursued; it was no sheep for sacrifice or shield of ox-hide for which they ran, but for the life of Hector, the tamer of horses. Thrice they ran round the city, and all the gods looked on.

And Zeus said: 'This is a piteous sight that I behold. My heart is grieved for Hector—Hector, who has ever worshipped me with sacrifice, for now the great Achilles is pursuing him round the walls of Troy. Come, ye gods, let us take counsel together. Shall we save him from death, or let him fall beneath the hand of Achilles?'

Then Athene said: 'What is this that thou sayest, great sire?—to rescue a man whom Fate has appointed to die? Do it, if it be thy will; but we, the other gods, approve it not.'

Zeus answered her: 'My heart is loath; yet be it as thou wilt.'

Then Athene came down in haste from the top of Olympus, and still Hector fled and Achilles pursued, just as a dog pursues a fawn upon the hills. And ever Hector made for the gates, or to get shelter beneath the towers, if haply those that stood upon them might defend him with their spears; and ever Achilles would get before him, and drive him towards the plain. So they ran, one making for the city, and the other driving him to the plain.

But as for Hector, Apollo even yet helped him, and gave him strength and nimble knees, else could he not have held out against Achilles, who was swiftest of foot among the sons of men.

When the two came in their running for the fourth time to the springs of Scamander, Zeus held out the great balance of doom, and in one scale he put the fate of Achilles, and in the other the fate of Hector; and lo! the scale of Hector sank down to the realms of death. And then Apollo left him.

Athene lighted down from the air close to Achilles and said: 'This, great Achilles, is our day of glory, for we shall slay Hector, mighty warrior though he be. For it is his doom to die, and not Apollo's self shall save him.'

Then the two chiefs came near to each other, and Achilles threw the mighty spear, but Hector saw it coming and avoided it, crouching on the ground, so that the spear flew above his head and fixed itself in the earth. But Athene snatched it from the ground and gave it back to Achilles, Hector not perceiving.

Then Hector threw his long-shafted spear. True aim he took, for the spear struck the very middle of Achilles' shield. It struck, but pierced it not, but bounded far away, for the shield was not of mortal make. And Hector stood dismayed, for he had not another spear. He knew that his end was come, and he said to himself: 'Now have the gods called me to my doom. Zeus and Apollo are with me no more; but if I must die, let me at least die in such a deed as men of after time may hear of.'

So he spake, and drew the mighty sword that hung by his side: then as an eagle rushes through the clouds to pounce on a leveret or a lamb, he rushed on the great Achilles. But he

188

dealt never a blow; for Achilles charged to meet him, his shield before his breast, his helmet bent forward as he ran, with the long plumes streaming behind, and the gleam of his spear-point was as the gleam of the evening star, which is the fairest of all the stars in heaven. One moment he thought where he should drive it home, for the armour which Hector had won from Patroclus guarded him well; but one spot there was, where by the collar-bone the neck joins the shoulder (and nowhere is the stroke of sword or spear more deadly). There he drove in the spear, and the point stood out behind the neck, and Hector fell in the dust.

Then Achilles cried aloud: 'Hector, thou thoughtest in the day when thou didst spoil Patroclus of his arms that thou wouldst be safe from vengeance, taking, forsooth, no account of me. And lo! thou art fallen before me, and now the dogs and vultures shall devour thee, but to him all the Greeks shall give due burial.'

But Hector, growing faint, spake to him: 'Nay, great Achilles, by thy life, and by thy knees, and by thy parents dear, I pray thee, let not the dogs of the Greeks devour me. Take rather the ransom, gold and bronze, that my father and mother shall pay thee, and let the sons and daughters of Troy give me burial rites.'

But Achilles scowled at him, and cried: 'Dog, seek not to entreat me! I could mince that flesh of thine and devour it raw, such grief hast thou brought me. No ransom, though it were ten times told, should buy thee back; no, not though Priam should offer thy weight in gold.'

Then Hector, who was now at the point to die, spake to him: 'I know thee well, what manner of man thou art, that the heart in thy breast is iron only. Only beware lest some vengeance from the gods come upon thee in the day when Paris and Apollo shall slay thee, for all thy valour, by the Scaean Gate.'

So speaking he died. But Achilles said, 'Die, hound. My fate I meet when Zeus and the other gods decree.'

Then he drew his spear out of the corpse, and stripped off

the arms; and all the Greeks came about the dead man, marvelling at his stature and beauty, and no man came but wounded the dead corpse. And one would say to another, 'Surely this Hector is less dreadful now than in the day when he would burn our ships with fire.'

Then Achilles devised a ruthless thing in his heart. He pierced the ankle-bones of Hector, and so bound the body with thongs of ox-hide to the chariot, letting the head drag behind, the head that once was so fair, and now was so disfigured in the dust. So he dragged Hector to the ships. And Priam saw him from the walls, and scarce could his sons keep him back, but that he should go forth and beg the body of his dear son from him who had slain him.

While the Trojans mourned for Hector in the city, the Greeks went back to the camp. All the others were scattered, each to his own ship, but Achilles spake to the Myrmidons, saying, 'Loose not your horses from the yoke, but let us do honour to Patroclus, driving our chariots round the dead, and making lamentation the while.'

Then the Myrmidons did as he had bidden them; thrice round the dead they drave their chariots, and made lamentation; and Achilles led the mourning. Also he laid the body of Hector in the dust beside the dead. After that he made a funeral feast for his people.

The next day they made a great pile of wood, and laid the body of Patroclus thereon. Nine dogs had the prince, and Achilles slew two of them on the pile, and four horses he slew, and he slew also twelve Trojan prisoners. And then he set fire to the pile.

And when the burning was well-nigh ended, Achilles spake, saying: 'Quench ye the fire that yet remains with wine, and gather the bones of Patroclus together where they lie apart in the midst of the pile, and put them in an urn of gold against the day of my death. And make over them a tomb not over large; but when I am dead also, then shall ye that are left make it higher, as is meet.'

Then when the rites were completed, that full honour might

be done to his dead friend, Achilles brought from his ship costly treasure as prizes for the funeral games. Then the men sat and watched while the great chiefs and the noblest warriors competed in a chariot race, in archery, in wrestling and in combat and boxing and in other sports. When the games of Patroclus were ended, the people scattered to the ships to eat and drink, and afterwards they slept. But Achilles slept not, for he remembered his dear Patroclus, and all that they two had done and endured together.

After the burial of Patroclus, the gods held council about Hector, for Achilles did despite to the body of Hector in dragging it about the tomb of his friend, but the gods had pity on the dead man, because in his life he had ever honoured them.

Then did Zeus send for Thetis, and when she was come to Olympus, he said: 'Get thee to the camp, and bid thy son give up Hector for ransom, for I am wroth with him because he doth dishonour the dead.'

So Thetis went to Achilles, and found him weeping softly for his dead friend, for the strength of his sorrow was now spent, and she said to him: 'It is the will of the gods that thou give up the body of Hector, and take in exchange the ransom of gold and precious things which his father will give thee for him.'

And her son answered, 'Be it so, if the gods will have it.'

Then Zeus sent Iris, as his messenger, to King Priam, where he sat with his face wrapped in his mantle, and his sons weeping about him, and his daughters wailing through the chambers of his palace.

Then Iris spake: 'Be of good cheer, Priam, son of Dardanus; Zeus has sent me to thee. Go, taking with thee such gifts as may best please the heart of Achilles, and bring back the body of thy dear son Hector. Go without fear of death or harm, and go alone. Only let an aged herald be with thee, to help thee when thou bringest back the body of the dead.'

Then Priam rose with joy, and bade his sons bring forth his chariot and a wagon.

He bade put into the wagon shawls and mantles that had never been washed, and rugs, and cloaks, and tunics, twelve of each, and ten talents of gold, and two bright three-footed cauldrons, and four basins, and a cup of passing beauty which the Thracians had given him.

The old man spared nothing that he had, if only he might buy back the body of his son.

Then Hecuba his wife, came near, and bade a woman-servant come and pour water on his hands. And after he had washed King Priam took a great cup from the hands of his wife, and made a libation to Zeus, and prayed:

'Hear me, Father Zeus, and grant that Achilles may pity me. And do thou send me now a lucky sign, that I may go with a good heart to the ships of the Greeks.'

And Zeus heard him, and sent an eagle, a mighty bird, whose wings spread out on either side as wide as is the door of some spacious chamber in a rich man's house. At Priam's right hand it flew high above the city, and all rejoiced when they saw the sign.

Then the old man mounted his chariot in haste, and drove forth from the palace. Before him the mules drew the four-wheeled wagon, and these the herald Idaeus guided. But his chariot the old king drove himself.

Zeus saw him depart, and said to Hermes: 'Hermes, go guide King Priam to the ships of the Greeks, so that no man see him before he comes to the tents of Achilles.'

Then Hermes fastened on his feet the fair sandals of gold with which he flies, fast as the wind, over sea and land, and in his hand he took the rod with which he opens and closes, as he wills, the eyes of men. And he flew down and lighted on the plain of Troy, taking on him the likeness of a fair youth.

But when Priam and his herald had driven past the great Tomb of Ilus, they stopped the horses and the mules, to let them drink of the river. And darkness came over the land; and then the herald spied Hermes, and said:

'Consider, my lord, what we shall do. I see a man, and I am

sore afraid lest he slay us. Shall we flee on the chariot, or shall we go near and entreat him, that he may have pity upon us?'

Then the old man was sore troubled, and his hair stood up with fear. But Hermes came near and took him by the hand and said:

'Whither goest thou, old man, with thy horses and mules through the darkness? Hast thou no fear of these fierce Greeks, who are close at hand? If anyone should see thee with all this wealth, what then? And thou art not young, nor is thy attendant young, that ye could defend yourselves against an enemy. But I will not harm thee, nor suffer any other, for thou art like my own dear father. I will guide thee to Achilles.'

Then he leapt into the chariot of the king and caught the reins in his hand, and gave the horses and the mules a strength that was not their own. And when they came to the ditch and the trench that guarded the ships, lo! the guards were busy with their meal; but Hermes made sleep descend upon them, and opened the gates, and brought in Priam with his treasures. And when they came to the tent of Achilles, Hermes lighted down from the chariot and said:

'Lo! I am Hermes, whom my Father Zeus hath sent to be thy guide. And now I shall depart, for I would not that Achilles should see me. But go thou in, and clasp his knees, and beseech him by his father, and his mother, and his child. So shalt thou move his heart with pity.'

So Hermes departed to Olympus, and King Priam came down from the chariot, leaving the herald to care for the horses and the mules, and went to the tent. There he found Achilles sitting; his comrades sat apart, but two waited on him, for he had but newly ended his meal, and the table was yet at his hand. But no man saw King Priam till he was close to Achilles, and caught his knees and kissed his hands, the dreadful, murderous hands that had slain so many of his sons. As a man who slays another by mishap flies to some stranger land, to some rich man's home, and all wonder to see him, so Achilles wondered to see King Priam, and his

193

còmrades wondered, looking one at another. Then King Priam spake:

'Think of thy father, godlike Achilles, and pity me. He is old, as I am, and, it may be, his neighbours trouble him, seeing that he has no defender; yet so long as he knows that thou art alive, it is well with him, for every day he hopes to see his dear son returned from Troy. But as for me, I am altogether wretched. Many a valiant son I had—nineteen born to me of one mother—and most of them are dead, and he that was the best of all, who kept our city safe, he has been slain by thee. He it is whom I have come to ransom. Have pity on him and on me, thinking of thy father. Never, surely, was lot so sad as this, to kiss the hands that slew a son.'

The words so stirred the heart of Achilles that he wept, thinking now of Patroclus, and now of his old father at home; and Priam wept, thinking of his dead Hector. But at last Achilles stood up from his seat and raised King Priam, having pity on his white hair and his white beard, and spake:

'How didst thou dare to come to the ships of the Greeks, to the man who slew thy sons? Surely, thou must have a heart of iron. But sit thou down: let our sorrows rest in our hearts, for there is no profit in lamentation. It is the will of the gods that men should suffer woe, though they are themselves free from care. Two chests are set by the side of Father Zeus, one of good and one of evil gifts, and he mixes the lot of men, taking out of both. Many noble gifts did the gods give to King Peleus: wealth and bliss beyond that of other men, and kingship over the Myrmidons. Ay! and they gave him a goddess to be his wife. But they gave also this evil, that he had no stock of stalwart children in his house, but one son only, and I cannot help him at all in his old age, for I tarry here far away in Troy. Thou, too, old man, hadst wealth and power of old, and lordship over all that lies between Lesbos and Phrygia and the stream of Hellespont. And to thee the gods have given this ill, that there is ever battle and slaughter about thy city walls. But as for thy son, wail not for him, for thou canst not raise him up.'

But Priam answered: 'Make me not to sit, great Achilles, while Hector lies unhonoured. Let me ransom him, and look upon him with my eyes, and do thou take the gifts. And the gods grant thee to return safe to thy fatherland.'

But Achilles frowned and said: 'Vex me not; I am minded myself to give thee back thy Hector. For my mother came from the sea, bearing the bidding of Zeus, and thou, methinks, hast not come hither without some guidance from the gods. But trouble me no more, lest I do thee some hurt.'

And King Priam feared and held his peace. Then Achilles hastened from his tent, and two comrades with him. First they loosed the horses from the chariot, and the mules from the wagon; then they brought in the herald Idaeus, and took the gifts. Only they left of them two cloaks and a tunic, wherein they might wrap the dead. And Achilles bade the women wash and anoint the body, but apart from the tent, lest, perchance, Priam should see his son and cry aloud, and so awaken the fury in his heart. But when it was washed and anointed, Achilles himself lifted the body in his arms and put it on the litter, and his comrades lifted the litter into the wagon.

And when all was finished, Achilles groaned and cried to his dead friend, saying:

'Be not wroth, Patroclus, if thou shouldst hear in the unknown land that I have ransomed Hector to his father; a noble ransom hath he paid me, and of this, too, thou shalt have thy share.'

He went back to his tent, and set himself down, over against Priam, and spake: 'Thy son is ransomed, old man, and tomorrow shalt thou see him and take him back to Troy. But now let us eat. Tomorrow shalt thou weep for Hector; many tears, I trow, shall be shed for him.'

So they ate and drank. And when the meal was ended, Achilles sat and marvelled at King Priam's noble look, and King Priam marvelled at Achilles, so strong he was and fair.

Then Priam said: 'Let me sleep, great Achilles. I have

not slept since my son fell by thy hand. Now I have eaten and drunk, and my eyes are heavy.'

So the comrades of Achilles made him a bed outside, where no one might see him, should it chance that any of the chiefs should come to the tent of Achilles to take counsel, and should espy him, and tell it to King Agamemnon.

But before he slept King Priam said: 'If thou art minded to let me bury Hector, let there be a truce between my people and the Greeks. For nine days let us mourn for Hector, and on the tenth will we bury him and feast the people, and on the eleventh raise a great tomb above him, and on the twelfth we will fight again, if fight we must.'

And Achilles answered, 'Be it so, I will stay the war for so long.'

Before dawn, while Priam slept, there came to him Hermes, the messenger of Zeus, who said: 'Sleepest thou, Priam, among thy foes? Achilles has taken ransom for thy Hector; but thy sons that are left would pay thrice as much for thee should Agamemnon hear that thou wert among the ships.'

The old man heard and trembled, and roused the herald, and the two yoked the horses and the mules. So they passed through the army, and no man knew. And when they came to the river, Hermes departed to Olympus, and the morning shone over all the earth.

It was Cassandra who first espied them as they came. Her father she saw, and the herald, and then the dead body on the litter, and she cried, 'Sons and daughters of Troy, go to meet Hector, if ever ye have met him with joy as he came back from the battle.'

And straightway there was not man or woman left in the city. They met the wagon when it was close to the gates, and they met it with weeping and wailing. King Priam spake:

'Let us pass; ye shall have enough of wailing when we have taken him to his home.'

So they took him to his home, and laid him on his bed. And the minstrels lamented, and the women wailed.

Then first of all came Andromache, his wife, and cried:

'O my husband, thou hast perished in thy youth, and I am left in widowhood, and our child, thy child and mine, is but an infant! I fear me he will not grow to manhood. Ere that day this city will fall, for thou art gone who wast its defender.'

Next spake Hecuba, his mother: 'Dear wast thou, my son, in life, to the immortal gods, and dear in death. Achilles dragged thee about the tomb of his dear Patroclus, but now thou liest fresh and fair as one whom the god of the golden bow has slain with sudden stroke.'

And last of all came Helen, and cried: 'Many a year has passed since I came to Troy—would that I had died before! And never have I heard from thy lips one bitter word. Therefore I weep for thee; no one is left to be my friend in all the broad streets of Troy. All shun and hate me now.'

Then Priam spake to those who crowded weeping by the palace gates: 'Go, my people, gather wood for the burial, and fear not any ambush of the Greeks, for Achilles promised that he would stay the war until the twelfth day should come.'

So for nine days the people gathered much wood, and on the tenth they laid Hector upon the pile, and lit fire beneath it. And when it was burnt they quenched the embers with wine. Then his brethren and comrades gathered together the white bones, and laid them in a chest of gold; and this they covered with purple robes and put in a great coffin, and laid upon it stones many and great. And over all they raised a mighty mound; and all the while the watchers watched, lest the Greeks should arise and slay them. Last of all was a great feast held in the palace of King Priam.

So they buried Hector, the tamer of horses.

Not many days after this Achilles himself perished, for, having declared at a banquet of the chiefs that he would make his way by his valour into Troy, he strove to break through the Scaean Gate. There did Paris, from behind, wound him to the death, with an arrow that bit deeply into his heel, but it was Apollo who guided the archer's hand.

Thus was the great warrior done to death by a coward; and

one who had violated the laws of hospitality and stolen another man's wife.

A fierce battle raged over the body of Achilles. It lasted the whole day till Zeus in pity sent a sandstorm to bring it to an end and the comrades of the lion-hearted warrior bore his body from the battlefield. It was washed with water and anointed with sweet spices and laid upon a bier. Then Thetis came to her son as he lay upon the bier, and with her came all the daughters of the sea, wailing and lamenting, and they put upon the body garments like unto those of the gods. The nine Muses came to sing the funeral dirge. Lovely was the sound of their voices answering each other; and there was not one of the Greeks but wept, so sweetly did they sing. For seventeen days and nights the lamentations of gods and men continued; and on the eighteenth day the body of Achilles was laid upon a huge pyre and the fire kindled. And in the morning when the fierce flames had died down, the bones were gathered up and placed in the golden amphora, Dionysus' wedding gift to Thetis and Peleus, and united with the bones of his friend Patroclus, as Achilles had wished. Then the whole army raised a tomb on a jutting rock on the shore, towering high, so that seafarers saw it from a great distance ever after.

Thetis brought prizes for the games, and never before were prizes so fair seen at any burying as those the silver-footed goddess set before the chiefs. And also his mother gave the arms of Achilles to be a prize to the bravest of the Greeks.

Then stood up Odysseus and Ajax the Greater, and contended together; but the Greeks adjudged the prize to Odysseus, therefore Ajax slew himself.

Such was the burying of Achilles. Never before in all the land of Greece had there been such a burying not even for a mighty king. And never before were the prizes for the funeral games so fair as the prizes silver-footed Thetis put before the chieftains of the host.

When all was done the Greeks came in force against the walls of Troy and Paris was deeply wounded by an arrow. But still the city stood. And when Paris died Priam did not give Helen back to Menelaus but married her to his son Deliphobus. Then Helen's heart turned to Menelaus and to her own country and she would have escaped to the Greeks but that a watch was set upon her. When Odysseus by craft entered Troy in the guise of a beggar and deceived all the people, save Helen only, she told him what he had come to discover: where the Palladium, the Luck of Troy, lay hidden, which was the city's greatest treasure. And she helped him take it when the next night he came with brave Diomedes crawling through the great drain up to the temple of Athene.

Yet though the Luck of Troy was stolen the city could not be taken.

Now when Troy still held out, a certain Epeius, Athene advising him, devised a device by which the city could be taken. Secretly the Greeks cut much wood and made a great horse, hollow in its belly where twenty warriors fully armed might lie concealed, with a trap-door fastening from within in its underside. Then the Greek armies made as if they had departed, burning their camp and sailing away in their ships to a nearby hiding-place. But the bravest of the chieftains, Odysseus, Menelaus, Diomedes, and their chosen companions, remained hidden inside the horse. This the Trojans drew with ropes into their city, first taking down the gate that it might enter. And the people sat round about while the Elders considered what they should do, and three counsels were given: the first was to cleave the wood, the second to drag the horse to the brow of the hill and cast it down, and the third to leave it as an offering to the gods. And the third counsel prevailed, for it was the doom of the city that it should perish by the horse.

But one test they made to quiet those who still feared the Greeks. Helen, able to speak with any voice, they forced to walk three times round the horse calling by name each of the Greek chiefs in the voices of their wives. So truly did she speak that the younger men would have revealed themselves, but the wise Odysseus saved the warriors by restraining them. Sure now that all was well, the Trojans drew the horse up to the citadel and, rejoicing, gave themselves to drinking and feasting, for they thought the war was ended. At night the chiefs came out from the horse and threw open the gates to the returned Greeks who entered and took the city.

With terrible savagery the Greeks took vengeance on the Trojans. They despoiled the citadel, killing without mercy the soldiers and the ordinary people of Troy, and even babes and young children. This inhuman cruelty caused great anger on Olympus, and Zeus permitted none of the Greek chieftains a quick and smooth passage home.

The Homecoming of Agamemnon

It was night, a winter's night, and the old watchman crouched on the palace roof at Argos. Peering through the darkness he scanned the night sky for the light which would let him know that Troy had fallen and his dear master was on the way home.

More than ten years had passed since Agamemnon, High King of Argos and Mycenae, sailed away in command of the expedition against Troy, to avenge the wrong done to his brother Menelaus, and his people longed for their king's return.

The watchman thought he saw a glimmer—was this what he was waiting for or only a bright star? He rubbed his eyes and peered into the gloom. Surely the light was growing stronger; yes, now it blazed in the darkness. It was the signal! The old man hurried down from the roof, calling the guards to rouse the household and inform Queen Clytemnestra that the war was over.

Lights appeared in the palace; there were cries of joy and sounds of activity, as the slaves ran from one to another passing on the news.

At dawn the citizens made thank offerings to the gods, and then gathered outside the king's house waiting for news. But there were those, in particular the City Elders, who were troubled in mind. They thought back on what had occurred in the kingdom while the king was away. First the terrible fate of Princess Iphigeneia. Her father had summoned her to Aulis —all thought for marriage with a prince—but the horrifying news had come that she was sacrificed on the altar of Artemis to appease the goddess whose displeasure had prevented the sailing of the fleet. The trusted guardian left by Agamemnon in charge of the queen's person had strangely disappeared, while Aegisthus, the king's cousin but avowed enemy, visited the city and was now living in the palace with the queen, and young Prince Orestes had been sent away.

All this the grave-faced Elders talked of amongst themselves. The queen had kept silent about her daughter's death, and none knew her feelings toward the king. But what was in her heart now that she knew of his homecoming?

'A curse lies on the house of Atreus,' murmured one old man, 'and has descended from father to son ever since the sin of Pelops.' And those who heard him shuddered, remembering the crime committed by Atreus, father of the king, against his own brother in causing him unknowingly to eat the flesh of his young children. A deed so horrible and impious that, it was said, the sun could not behold it and turned his back.

The queen came from the palace and went directly to the temple to render public thanksgiving to Zeus, and show to the people the aspect of a true and loving wife. Then she explained that a chain of beacons had flashed the news of victory from Mount Ida of Troy, to the island of Lemnos, and then from hill to hill in Greece until the message reached Argos. She bade them all render thanks to the gods for their king's safety and his glorious victory.

But, in truth, Clytemnestra dissembled. She hid her black hatred for Agamemnon, and gave no hint of the evil that awaited his return. It was Aegisthus who had planned the beacon fires to give them full warning of his coming.

All knew that ships could not follow quickly on the beacons' signal and many wondered if the message were true. But after some lapse of time a travel-stained, exhausted herald staggered up the dusty road and announced that Agamemnon's ships had safely come to shore. The man fell on his knees and kissed the ground. He said he had not thought ever to see his homeland again. He told the people, who clustered round him eager for news, about the sufferings of the soldiers during the weary siege of Troy, and of their perilous homeward journey—during which the ships of Menelaus had been scattered by a great storm and were not seen again. The people, praising their victorious lord, hurried to welcome him.

Agamemnon came up with his men in procession from the harbour. The excited people would have crowded round his chariot and impeded his progress if the bodyguard had not held them back and cleared a way through to the palace.

In the procession the king, calm and dignified, rode in the first chariot. Following was a chariot bearing Princess Cassandra, daughter of old Priam; she was the Award of Honour to Agamemnon. After her came wagons loaded with the spoils of war from Troy, the chariots of Agamemnon's troop commanders, and then the long line of spearmen and archers. These marched more eagerly now that they were in sight of their homes. But among the cheering crowd were many women who looked in vain for husbands, sons and brothers.

The king's chariot stopped by the palace steps. The leader of the Council advanced to greet his lord, 'All hail, O King! No honour we accord thee can match thy glorious victory for no praise is great enough for Ilium's conqueror. But in love and reverence we bid thee welcome home to thy kingdom.' The crowd roared their welcome in support of the Elder's formal speech. The king stood and addressed his people, 'To Argos and the gods all hail in the happiness of this home-coming! Let our thanks be as great as our glory in the victory over Troy. First to the gods I make thanksgiving and then will I call an assembly to inquire into the affairs of my people. Those who have suffered will be comforted and cared for, and those who have sinned against god and man will be judged.'

Queen Clytemnestra now came out to the palace steps, magnificent in her robes, and accompanied by her maidens. With both arms outstretched, she greeted Agamemnon and cried, 'Hail to thee my lord, with love I welcome thee, and rejoice that dread fear is now lifted from my heart.' Turning to the Elders she said, 'I think it no shame to lay my passion bare before all eyes.' And hysterically she spoke of her lonely terror during the intolerable years of war; of her anxiety and suffering on account of the king's danger, and now of her thankfulness at his safe return.

She explained to Agamemnon that Orestes was in faraway Phocis where she had sent him for safety, and then she entreated the king to come to her loving embrace. She ordered her slaves to lay a gold and purple carpet from his chariot to the doorway of the palace, and called on him to descend. Agamemnon said, 'Do not tempt the gods with an honour due to them. This broidered pathway is not for mortal man but for gods.' But Clytemnestra continued to press him and, using flattery, said, 'When a great conqueror yields to woman's wish that is grace indeed.' And so she persuaded Agamemnon. He called for a servant to unloose the straps and remove his shoes, and coming down from his chariot he walked on the tapestried path into the palace, the people kneeling in reverence as he passed.

Meanwhile Cassandra, dressed as a prophetess, sat in silence, apprehensively fingering the folds of her long white cloak. Clytemnestra reappeared and called to her. 'You! Come in also. I speak to you, Cassandra.' Cassandra stared straight ahead as though she had not heard. The queen called again, but still had no response.

Clytemnestra had been outraged that her husband brought the Trojan princess home with him, but hid her feelings in his presence. Now her bitter resentment was revealed. She shouted to Cassandra: 'Get down! I am speaking to you. Get down, and follow me. The gods sent you here as a slave, so no insolence. Be thankful you are come to a household of high repute, where thralls are treated with kindness.' Cassandra, trembling violently, still kept silent. The queen, exasperated, went back into the palace.

Then Cassandra's trembling suddenly ceased. She became rigid in the grip of a prophetic trance.

'Otototoi . . . dreams . . . dreams,' she murmured. Then

wild, incoherent cries fell from her lips, her unseeing eyes
were glazed with horror, she shuddered as she tried to reveal
the terror that now possessed her. 'What are those shadows
that move before my eyes . . . the shapes of little children . . .
murdered by the hand of one who loves them . . . the steaming
dish of baked meats. O! horrible, horrible . . . their father
eats.'

Then she spoke more quickly, though still in faltering
Greek, and struggling for expression. 'That vile deed yet calls
for vengeance. And woe to this house that has earned the
loathing of the gods. Evil reigns in it once more: and danger,
water . . . water, danger and death. You shall see Agamemnon
dead!'

Cassandra cried aloud in the agony of her vision, while
the mystified Elders looked at each other in dismay. One
said, 'I heard, but can find no clue.' And another muttered,
'But how could such a deed be done? I see no way.'

Then Cassandra cried, 'Aaaah . . . there is a hand, and
another hand that reaches gropingly. Ohh . . . blood and

treachery. All comes so quick. And the fire of death, it moves . . . it comes at me . . . the rending blade . . . I too shall die. The thing which must be shall be. Soon you shall sorrow for these deeds, and confess me all too true a seer.'

In the last violence of her trance Cassandra tore off her prophetic robe and trampled it underfoot, crying, 'This stuff of prophecy I shall use no more.' Then calmly she turned to face the crowd, 'Why should I grieve?' she said, 'I saw the fall of Troy where men destroyed my father. I go to drink my cup and will endure to die.' She stepped down from the chariot and went into the palace, crying as she entered, 'All hail to you, Death Gates!' Then the great door was shut.

Inside the palace slaves were busy preparing a feast to celebrate the king's return. A bath had been made ready for Agamemnon, to revive his tired body and wash away the stains of travel. Fresh garments were laid out, and Clytemnestra stood nearby. When he stepped from the bath she came forward as if to give him a towel. Instead she enmeshed him in a net-like robe, and Aegisthus, bursting into the room, attacked the helpless king with his sword.

'Help! Treason! I am murdered!' shouted Agamemnon. But his wife seized an axe and struck him again and yet again, so that he fell back dead into the silver-sided bath.

Aegisthus and Clytemnestra killed Cassandra too, and threw her body on top of the king. The soldiers Aegisthus had in hiding quickly overpowered Agamemnon's loyal servants, and soon all was quiet in the palace.

Indistinct cries and groans were heard by the Elders as they stood outside. The bemused old men had hardly decided what to do when the palace doors were flung open and Clytemnestra stood before their horrified eyes: a bloody axe in her hand, and blood on her face and clothes. In a frenzy of wild triumph she cried, 'Agamemnon your king and my husband is dead! By me he fell and by me he died! Dead too is his Trojan princess. Now is my child revenged!' Then, the fire gone out of her, she sank back against the door frame. Behind her stood Aegisthus, flushed and triumphant. A company of his spearmen appearing from either side came down into the square to dominate the crowd. Aegisthus also had had his revenge. Agamemnon was dead, and he insolently announced his union with the queen.

The hastily assembled soldiers of Argos were no match for the usurper's well-prepared troops; they, and the shocked, submissive people, were quiet when Clytemnestra, supported by the arm of her lover, announced that since Orestes was not there, she and Aegisthus would assume the kingship and rule together. This they did for nearly seven years.

But the story did not end there. Orestes, now grown to manhood, went to Apollo's shrine at Delphi to ask the oracle if he should avenge the murder of his father. The god commanded him to do so. With his closest friend, Pylades, both wearing disguise, Orestes went to Argos and found his father's tomb outside the city walls. After praying, he cut off a long strand of hair, and had just laid it, his first offering, on the tomb when he saw a crowd of women coming that way.

The two young men hid in a thicket from where they could watch unseen. The mourning women were led by Electra, the dead king's daughter, who placed offerings around the tomb, and afterwards prayed aloud: for pity on her condition under the usurping tyrant; for power to avenge her father's death; and for the restoring of the kingdom to Orestes. Then she caught sight of the beribboned tress of hair. Excitedly she showed it to her companions, who wondered how it came there, and by whose hand. 'Think—who besides myself would leave this sign of grief upon my father's tomb?' said Electra. 'And is it not wonderfully like my hair?' Hopefully she looked about her, but seeing no one, covered her face with her hands and wept, 'O, Orestes! If you were but beside me to strengthen my weakness!'

Then Orestes came and stood near to his sister. Startled, Electra looked up at the seeming stranger. He spoke. 'Your prayers have been answered,' he said. 'Hereafter give thanks to the gods.' 'What do you mean?' asked Electra. 'What have the gods done for me?' 'They have shown you the face you longed to see,' said Orestes. 'Whose face is that?' she asked, hardly daring to hope. 'Orestes',' was the answer. Electra looked searchingly at him and then threw herself into her brother's arms.

Together with Pylades, they now planned to avenge the death of Agamemnon. Orestes went to the palace, pretending that he and Pylades were wayfarers who had proof of the death of Orestes. Queen Clytemnestra was delighted to hear this news and sent a messenger to summon Aegisthus. When he came Orestes drew his sword and cut him down. Then, despite his mother's pleas for mercy and forgiveness, Orestes killed her too.

Now, because he had slain his mother, even though it was in obedience to Apollo's oracle, Orestes brought down on himself the vengeance of the terrible Furies, who pursued all who killed members of their own family. The Furies followed Orestes wherever he went, they were with him by day and by night, he could not be rid of them. Even in the shrine at Delphi, where he despairingly sought cleansing from his blood-guilt, they persecuted him. At last Apollo had pity. He bade Orestes go to the temple of Athene in Athens where Zeus was willing for his case to be heard before a panel of upright citizens. Hermes led Orestes to Athens where Apollo and Athene argued with the Furies on his behalf. At the end there was an equal number for and against. It was the goddess who had the casting vote and she prevailed upon the Furies to set Orestes free. From that time onwards the Furies were spoken of as the Eumenides—the 'Kindly Ones'.

To fully expiate his crime Apollo gave Orestes one last command. He was to fetch the image of Artemis from the temple on the rocky coast of Tauris, and bring it back to Greece.

Faithful Pylades went with Orestes on this dangerous undertaking. They came safely to the temple, but then were captured, and, as was the custom, the priestess came to prepare them for the death that was the fate of all strangers.

Now, this priestess was none other than Orestes' sister Iphigeneia. Her father had indeed been forced to let her be the victim for sacrifice, but she was saved at the last moment by Artemis, who brought her to this lonely place. Brother and sister recognised each other with great joy. Iphigeneia made it possible for Orestes and Pylades to take the statue of Artemis and then she arranged escape for them all.

After their return to Greece the statue of the goddess was put in the newly built temple of Artemis at Brauron, a city not far from Athens; and there Iphigeneia became Chief Priestess for the rest of her life. Orestes, having now propitiated the gods, became, as was his father before him, king of Argos and Mycenae. He married his cousin Hermione, and, finding that they had long loved each other, gave Electra in marriage to his friend Pylades.

So the children of Agamemnon were at last set free from the curse which had sorely afflicted their family, and the house of Atreus found happiness and peace.

Odysseus and Circe

Leaving Troy a smoking ruin, the Greek kings and chieftains departed for their homes. But few escaped storm and shipwreck, and fewer still came safely to their own kingdoms. Zeus allowed none of the Greek princes to return home in triumph with the spoils of war, so great was the anger against them in Olympus for their cruelty in the streets of Troy. Of them all Odysseus was longest on the way, and after nine years at sea he was still far from Ithaca.

Odysseus and his men sailed from Troy in twelve ships. Immediately they ran into fierce storms and were blown off course. They were captured by the Cyclops, Polyphemus, who slaughtered several of the men, the rest only escaping death by a clever ruse, and by destroying his one eye. Dire catastrophe overtook them at Lamos, where the inhabitants, giant cannibals, crushed the ships and captured the crews. Odysseus' own ship, being farthest out in the harbour, was the sole survivor.

The single ship sailed on to the island of Aea, where Circe the enchantress dwelt. She was a haughty beauty, with hair like the sun, and was deeply skilled in magic. Odysseus did not know what country they had reached, nor that it was the abode of Circe, but, since all his men were sorely in need of rest, he anchored in a sheltered bay.

In the little harbour a dispute arose among the men as to which of them should go ashore and explore the country; for there was a necessity that some should go to procure more water and provisions, their stock of both being well nigh spent. But their hearts failed them when they called to mind the shocking fate of their fellows whom the cannibal

Laestrygonians had eaten, and those whom the foul Cyclops Polyphemus had crushed between his jaws; which moved them so tenderly in the recollection that they wept. But tears never yet supplied any man's wants; this Odysseus knew full well, and so, dividing his men into two parties—at the head of the first he put himself, and at the head of the other Eurylochus, a man of tried courage—he cast lots which of them should go up into the country. And the lot fell upon Eurylochus and his company, two and twenty in number, and they took their leave, with tears, of Odysseus and the men who stayed. And the eyes of those that stayed were the same wet badges of weak humanity, for they surely thought never to see these their companions again, being now sure that on every coast where they should come, they would find nothing but cannibals and savages.

Eurylochus and his party proceeded up the country, till in a dale they descried the great house of Circe, built of bright stone, by the road's side. Before her gate lay many beasts— such as wolves, lions, leopards—which, by her art, of wild she had rendered tame. These arose when they saw strangers, and ramped upon their hinder paws, and fawned upon Eurylochus and his men, who dreaded the effects of such monstrous kindness. Staying at the gate they then heard the sound of singing. For within the enchantress sat at her loom, and sang such strains as suspended all mortal faculties, while she wove a web, subtle and glorious, and of texture inimitable on earth. Strains so ravishingly sweet provoked even the sagest and most prudent heads among the party to knock and call at the gate. The shining gate the enchantress opened, and bade them come in and feast. They, unwise, followed her, all but Eurylochus, who stayed without the gate, suspicious that some trap was laid for them.

Being entered, Circe placed the men in chairs of state, and set before them meal and honey, and Smyrna wine; but she had mixed with the wine baleful drugs of powerful enchant-ment. When they had eaten, and drunk of her cup, she touched them with her charming-rod, and straight they were

transformed into swine, having the bodies of swine, the bristles
and snout and grunting noises of that animal; only they still
retained the minds of men, which made them the more to
lament their brutish transformation. Having changed them she
drove them out, and shut them up in her sty with many more
whom her wicked sorceries had formerly changed, and gave
them swine's food—mast and acorns and chestnuts—to eat.

Eurylochus, who could not see these sad changes from
where he stood without the gate, when his companions did
not return thought they had all vanished by witchcraft, and
hurried back to the ship. He was so frightened and perplexed
that he could give no distinct report of anything. He remembered only a palace, and a woman singing at her work,
and gates guarded by lions. But his companions, he said,
were all vanished.

Then Odysseus, suspecting some foul witchcraft, snatched
his sword and his bow, and commanded Eurylochus instantly
to lead him to the place. But Eurylochus fell down and
embraced his knees, and besought him not to expose his

safety, and the safety of them all, to certain destruction.

'Do thou then stay, Eurylochus,' answered Odysseus, 'eat thou and drink in the ship in safety; while I go alone upon this adventure; necessity, from whose law there is no appeal, compels me.' So saying he quitted the ship and went on shore, accompanied by none. None had the hardihood to offer to share that perilous adventure with him, so much they dreaded the enchantments of the witch.

So singly Odysseus pursued his journey till he came to the shining gates which stood before Circe's mansion. But when he was about to put his foot over her threshold, he was suddenly stopped by the apparition of a young man bearing a golden rod in his hand, who was the god Hermes. He held Odysseus by the wrist to stay his entrance. 'Whither wouldst thou go?' he said. 'O, thou most wayward of the sons of men! Knowest thou not that this is the house of great Circe, where she keeps thy friends in a loathsome sty, changed from the fair forms of men into the detestable and ugly shapes of swine? Art thou prepared to share their fate, from which nothing can ransom thee?'

But neither the words of the god nor his coming from heaven could stop the daring foot of Odysseus, whose compassion for the misfortune of his friends rendered careless of danger. When Hermes perceived this, he had pity to see valour so misplaced, and he gave Odysseus the flower of the herb called moly, which is sovereign against enchantment. 'Take this in thy hand,' he said, 'and with it boldly enter the gates of the enchantress. When she shall strike thee with her rod, thinking to change thee, as she has changed thy friends, advance on her with thy sword, and extort from her the dreadful oath of the gods that she will use no enchantment against thee: then force her to restore thy abused companions.' Then, having instructed Odysseus how to use the little white flower, Hermes vanished.

When the god had departed, Odysseus with loud knockings beat at the gates of the palace. The shining gates were opened and great Circe invited in her guest. She seated him with more distinction than she had used to his fellows, and she mingled wine, mixed with those poisonous drugs, in a costly bowl, and he drank of it. When he had drunk, she struck him with her charming-rod, and 'To your sty!' she cried. 'Out, and join your companions.' But the preservative Hermes had given him was proof against these words, and Odysseus remained unchanged; then, as the god had directed him, he boldly charged the witch with his sword, as if he meant to take her life.

When Circe saw that her charms were powerless she cried out, and knelt beneath his sword, and clasping him about the knees, said, 'Who, or what manner of man art thou? Never has any man before drunk of this cup, but he repented of it in some brute's form. Thy shape remains as unaltered as thy mind. Thou canst be none other than Odysseus, renowned in all the world above all others for wisdom, whom the Fates have long decreed that I must love.'

'O Circe,' he replied, 'how darest thou speak of love to one whose friends thou hast turned into beasts? Thou must swear that thou wilt never attempt against me the treasons thou has practised against my companions.' The enchantress, won by the terror of his threats, or by the violence of that love for him she felt kindling in her veins, swore by Styx, the great oath of the gods, that she meditated no evil against him. Then Odysseus made show of gentler treatment, which gave her hopes of inspiring him with love for her. She called her handmaids to deck her apartments, to spread rich carpets, and to set out her silver tables with dishes of the purest gold, and to do honour to her guest. One brought water to wash his feet, and one brought wine to chase away, with a refreshing sweetness, the sorrows that had come of late so thick upon him. After he had bathed in water scented with the choicest aromatics, they brought him rich apparel to put on. Then he was conducted to a throne of massive silver, and food fit for Zeus was placed before him. But the feast Odysseus desired was to see his friends (the partners of his voyage) once more in their own shape; the food which could give him nourishment was that which he could take in with his eyes. Lacking this glad sight he sat melancholy and thoughtful, and would taste none of the rich delicacies set before him.

Circe easily divined the cause of his sadness, and, leaving the place where she sat enthroned, went to the sty, and let abroad Odysseus' men, who came in like swine, and filled the ample hall where he sat with gruntings. But hardly had he time to take in their brutal metamorphosis, than, because of an ointment that Circe smeared over them, their bristles fell off and they were in their own shape again. They knew their leader and clung to him, rejoicing in their restoration but with some shame for their late change; and wept so loud, blubbering out their joy in broken accents, that the palace was filled with the sound of pleasing mourning, and the witch herself was not unmoved at the sight. To make her atonement complete, she sent for the men who had stayed behind at the ship. Having given up their great commander for lost, when they saw him again they joined with their fellows crowding around him and even cried out with rapture; no expression can tell the joy they felt. Only Eurylochus would hardly be persuaded to enter that palace of wonders, for he remembered with a kind of horror how his companions had vanished from his sight.

The great Circe spake, and gave orders that there should be no more sadness among them, nor remembering of past sufferings. For as yet they fared like men that are exiles from their country, and if a gleam of mirth shot among them, it was suddenly quenched with the thought of their helpless and homeless condition.

Circe's kind persuasions wrought upon Odysseus and the rest, and they spent twelve months with her in her palace, experiencing many delights. The beautiful sorceress could contrive magical diversions, to 'fetch the day about from sun to sun, and rock the tedious year as in a delightful dream'.

Then at the end of that enchanted year Odysseus awoke as it were from a trance, and the thought of home returned with tenfold vigour to goad him; that home where he had left his virtuous wife Penelope, and his young son. Circe knew it was not within her power to detain him further, and placed no obstacles to his leaving. So at length, after many preparations, the time for departure being come, they set their sails, and took leave of Circe, who by her art calmed the heavens, and gave them smooth seas, and a right fore-wind (the seaman's friend) to bear them once more on their way.

The Wanderings of Aeneas

Greek soldiers, from the Wooden Horse and from the hidden Greek ships, had surprised the Trojans and were burning Troy, house by house. Priam, the king, was dead, dragged from the altar of Zeus, and murdered in front of his wife. Many of the Trojan heroes, in a last effort to save their city, perished in a combat they knew to be hopeless. Aeneas was fighting among them, but when Priam was killed his thoughts turned to his own wife and child and his old father. Suddenly his mother, the goddess Aphrodite, appeared before him. It was his duty, she said, to escape with his family to another country. She led him through the fire and slaughter safely to his own house.

At first Aeneas' father, who was old and very lame, felt he had lived his life and refused to leave Troy. But when the hair on the head of his little grandson seemed to burst into flame, and he saw a shooting star fall among the trees of Mount Ida, Anchises accepted these wonders as a sign from the gods, and agreed to leave. Aeneas, taking his father on his back and holding his son by the hand, led his wife and servants, carrying the images of the family gods and other treasures, out of the house. Keeping to the shadows, by lanes and by-ways they at last made their escape through the city gates. Then Aeneas discovered his wife was not with them. Fearing she had become lost in the crowds he went back to look for her. When her ghost appeared, he realised she had been killed, and was lost to him for ever; but her spirit spoke, consoling him. She told him not to grieve but to escape to fulfil his destiny. 'Your fate, my dear husband,' she said, 'is to cross the sea to Italy, where, by the river Tiber, you will found a new kingdom and take a new wife to be your queen.'

Aeneas, his household, and other refugees from Troy spent the winter months camping on the wooded slopes of Mount Ida. They cut down trees and built as many ships as were needed for all the company. When the little fleet of twenty ships was ready they set course for the north-west in search of the new land.

First they put in at a harbour in Thrace, but finding that the king of that country had murdered a former companion of Aeneas, they sailed south to the little island of Delos, where Apollo and Artemis had been born. In the temple of Apollo, the voice of the oracle spoke to them in these words:

'Go and look for your ancient mother!'

Temple prophecies were often puzzling, and the voyagers tried to guess what the oracle could mean. Anchises said that their 'ancient mother' must be Crete, the island of their ancestors, where there was another Mount Ida. So the ships sailed still further south, to Crete. Here they began to lay the foundations of their city but their work was not blessed: a plague broke out, crops withered, animals sickened and died. In this desperate state Anchises urged Aeneas to go to the nearest temple of Apollo for advice. But that night the images of the gods they had brought from Troy appeared beside his bed and spoke to Aeneas, giving him a message from Apollo. They were wrong in thinking Crete their destined home. They must leave it and sail to Italy, where the Trojan race had come from long ago.

So far the voyagers had been sailing among the beautiful Aegean islands, but now they turned west, round the south of Greece, into the Ionian Sea. A storm which lasted three days drove the ships off course and on to the shore of an unknown island. While the exhausted Trojans were eating the roasted flesh of ox and goat, taken from herds browsing in the flat fields, terrible, evil-smelling, monstrous birds with girls' faces and long talons, swooped over them and carried off the food. They did this again and again and could not be driven

away. The weary travellers could neither eat nor rest. These creatures, the Harpies, took their food, and the stench from their bodies was overwhelming. Unwittingly Aeneas and his companions had landed on one of the Strophades. These islands belonged to the Harpies and so did the animals the Trojans had slain for food. Celano, who led the Harpies, screamed from a rock the prophecy that before their journey was over and they built their new city the voyagers would be so tormented by hunger that they would even eat the platters their food had been on. Aeneas and his companions lost no time in taking to the ships and leaving that vile place.

Past the island of Ithaca they sailed, and on to Epirus, where they found Helenus, a son of King Priam of Troy. He refreshed the travellers and refitted the ships. Apollo had appeared to Helenus and given him a message for Aeneas:

'Many adventures and hardships still lie ahead of you, Aeneas, and Italy is a greater distance from you than you think. You will have travelled long, seen strange sights and endured much before you find, by a quiet river, a great white sow with thirty piglets and know that you have come to the end of your wanderings.

'Sail always with caution so that you may avoid the hazards ever at hand to entrap unwary seamen; and on unknown seas keep away from the shores, where the savage people attack travellers.

'But, when you come to the western coast of Italy, be certain, no matter how this delay irks your companions, to go to the Sybil's cave at Cumae. She will tell you the secrets of your future.

'I counsel you to pay homage to Hera. Pray to her and make sacrifices at her altars, wherever you come to them, for her enmity can do you great harm.'

Taking leave of kind Helenus, and laden with gifts, Aeneas and his companions set out once more. Early one morning they passed close to Mount Etna, the ever-smoking volcano. Resting on their oars the voyagers looked in fear and wonder. Black clouds of smoke and spurts of sudden flame issued from the great mass of rock, and strange rumbling sounds too. It was a terrifying sight. Then they saw the huge Cyclops Polyphemus, whom Odysseus had blinded, coming amongst the ships, the water reaching not much above his knees. He had waded into the sea to wash his eye-socket. He heard the sudden sound of oars as the sailors backed away from him and, shouting to his brother Cyclops for help, he reached around him with his vast arms, trying to grasp ship's prow or oar. Using all their strength the rowers pulled away, and Aeneas and every one of his ships managed to escape before the other giants came.

Round the south of Sicily they sailed and then steered north towards the mainland of Italy, but on the way old Anchises died, and he was buried on the island of Sicily, where an old friend and countryman of Aeneas was king.

Hera, wife of Zeus and Queen of Heaven, had no love for Aeneas or for any Trojan because his mother, the goddess Aphrodite, had been given the 'Apple for the Fairest' by Paris, prince of Troy. So, all through his life, Hera made

trouble for him. At this stage of the voyage, she was determined to hinder the ships. She went to Aeolus, god of the winds, to ask a favour of him. He granted it and at once freed all the rough winds from the bag in which they were kept. A terrible storm scattered the little fleet, wrecked most of the ships, and drove the rest ashore. Poseidon rose up in the spray of the storm to find out what was interfering with his waves. He ordered the winds to stop blowing and disturbing his sea, and asked the sea-nymphs to help him push the ships off the rocks and sandbanks. Using his trident, Poseidon himself pushed Aeneas' ship back into deep water.

The winds died down and, on a calm sea, the ships that were still with Aeneas—and few they were out of the twenty which had left the Trojan shore—made their way towards the nearest land, where they rested in a sheltered harbour.

During the storm Aphrodite, Aeneas' mother, had complained to Zeus. Why did he allow Hera to persecute her son?

'Don't be afraid for your son's safety,' said Zeus, smiling. 'He will survive. Let me tell you his destiny. For three years, Aeneas must fight wars in Italy. After that, Ascanius his son, changing his name to Iulus, will rule for thirty years. He will be the founder of a mighty city. Hundreds of years will pass and then a priestess of his line will become the mother of twins, Romulus and Remus. Romulus will build Rome, and name the city after himself. Hera may lessen her hatred of Aeneas to some degree, but only when Rome is a city will she become helpful to the people of the country. Centuries are of no account to us, the gods, so have patience.'

Zeus now sent Hermes down to earth, to Carthage the chief city of the North African country where Aeneas had taken refuge, to make sure he was received in a friendly way by the fierce inhabitants, whose Queen Dido was a favourite of the goddesss Hera. Aphrodite also came down and, dressed as a huntress, met her son to tell him about the queen. For a moment, before she vanished, she appeared in her divine form, and Aeneas recognised his mother. She made him invisible and so, unseen, he went on to Carthage and into Hera's temple. Among the sculptures on the walls of the temple telling the story of Troy, Aeneas recognised one of himself.

Queen Dido entered the temple and sat on the throne. The guards brought in a group of strangers: to the astonishment of Aeneas they were some of his friends from the ships he thought had been lost. They told their story, and asked permission to stay while they did repairs. The queen heard them graciously, and promised to help. 'But I am sorry your leader Aeneas himself is not here,' she said.

Sure now that he was welcome, Aphrodite let Aeneas become visible. Dido greeted him with warm sympathy. 'Being well acquainted with grief myself,' she said, 'I have pity for the misfortunes of others.' She ordered food and wine to be carried to the sailors in the harbour, and invited Aeneas and his friends to a banquet in her palace.

Then Aeneas sent a messenger to the ships to fetch gifts for the queen, and to bring young Ascanius to the palace. But Aphrodite, to protect Aeneas from any plot of Hera's and to make Queen Dido fall in love with him, disguised her son Eros as Ascanius and sent the little god of love to the banquet. Everyone thought he was Aeneas' son, and marvelled at his charm and beauty.

The disguised Eros sat between the queen and Aeneas and during the feast filled Dido's heart with love for her guest. Even Hera was strangely pleased when this happened, for she knew it should delay the journey of Aeneas for some time. For once, Hera and Aphrodite were in agreement. But when a year had passed and Aeneas still remained in Carthage, enjoying the queen's friendship, Zeus became annoyed by this delay.

He sent Hermes to Aeneas.

'You are forgetting your destiny, Aeneas. You must take Ascanius to Italy. This is the will of Zeus.'

Broken-hearted, Queen Dido watched Aeneas and the Trojans depart. She prepared a huge pyre, on which she put an image of Aeneas, and also his sword and shield. With the sword, the queen killed herself on the pyre. She hoped that, as the great fire burned, Aeneas would see the flames from far across the sea, and grieve for her death.

Not many days out from Carthage the little fleet ran into a fierce storm. Palinurus, the helmsman, told Aeneas it would be folly to try to sail on, and he suggested they take refuge in a Sicilian harbour. Aeneas agreed and said, 'That would please me well, for it is now the anniversary of my father's death, and it is right that I should make offerings at his tomb.'

The Trojans were made welcome by their old friend, the king of Sicily, and the next day Aeneas told them that the sacrifice and oblations to his father's grave would be followed by funeral games. Then, wearing, as was the custom, a wreath of myrtle leaves, Aeneas went to the tomb of Anchises, and poured out the libations: two cups of milk, two cups of wine and two cups of bullock's blood. A snake crawled from behind the grave and drank all the offerings, which was a sign that they had been accepted by the spirit of Anchises.

After a time of feasting the contests began: rowing, running, boxing, archery, and for the boys a mimic war. During these games, when the men were all occupied, Hera saw her chance to cause trouble. She sent Iris, her messenger, by way of the rainbow to Sicily where, changing her appearance, she mingled with the Trojan women and talked excitedly to them.

'Women of Troy! We have been travelling now for seven years. We are tired of the sea, and the ships are a prison. Let's burn them all, so that we can stay here in Sicily!'

The disguised Iris threw the first torch, and some of the women followed her example. Many ships were alight and it seemed too late to save them, but Aeneas prayed to Zeus for help, and the Father of the gods sent down a heavy shower of rain. Only four ships were lost before the fire was put out.

So Aeneas built a temple to Aphrodite and a new city for the women and children, the old men, and any others who wished to remain behind. Then he and the rest of the ships sailed away.

'Make his journey safe!' begged Aphrodite, and Poseidon agreed. 'But,' he said, 'I demand one sacrifice for the gods!'

That night, Palinurus the helmsman fell asleep on watch and, when the ship heeled over, he slid into the sea and was drowned. This sacrifice ensured the safety of the rest and they soon reached Cumae.

A white marble temple to Apollo stood high on the cliff. Beside the temple a cavern had been deeply cut in the rock and from here the famous Sybil shouted her oracles, which came up in a hundred voices, echoing through the hundred passages which led from her underground cave. The Sybil told Aeneas to pray to Apollo for a true prophecy. Then suddenly she began to rave in frenzy as the power of the god possessed her and spoke from her mouth:

'O gallant Aeneas, at last after many perils you have come safe to Cumae; so too shall you come safe to Latium but there trouble awaits you and a terrible war. The river Tiber will flow red with blood. Nor will Hera cease to persecute you. As Helen brought calamity to Troy, so here too marriage with a foreign bride will be a source of affliction. But be resolute. A happy turn in your fortunes comes when you least expect it with help from a Greek city.'

Then the Sybil was silent and her frenzy ceased.

Aeneas said that the prospect of further trials did not daunt him, but that he had a favour to ask. 'May I visit the shade of my dear father in the Lower World of the Dead? If Orpheus could safely make the journey and return, and Polydeuces and Theseus and Heracles too, may not I, the son of golden Aphrodite, be conducted thither?'

'Easy is the descent to the Underworld,' answered the Sybil. 'The difficulty is to return again to the sweet upper air. But there is a way there from nearby Lake Avernus, and in the dark woods surrounding the lake grows a certain tree which has among its branches one single golden bough. If you, Aeneas, can pluck this golden bough Fate is with you, and you may safely make the journey and return.'

Two of Aphrodite's doves led Aeneas to the tree by the lake, and perched beside the golden bough. Aeneas broke off the bough—which we call mistletoe—and brought it back to the Sybil.

First, sacrifices were made to the rulers of the Country of the Dead, and then Aeneas followed the Sybil below the ground. Looking about him as they went along the path which led to the Lower World Aeneas saw many of the horrific creatures of legend—Hydra, the monster slain by Heracles; the

Chimaera, which had the head of a lion, the hinder parts of a dragon, the body of a huge goat with scales and bristles, and a fiery breath; and the Gorgons, one of whom—Medusa—had snakes on her head, fangs for teeth, and eyes that turned men to stone; and the dreadful hundred-handed giant, Briareus.

When they came to the river Styx, over which Charon ferries the dead, Aeneas was sorely troubled to see a miserable crowd of spirits on the marshy bank, who jostled and surged forward trying to get on to the ferry. Every time they came near Charon pushed them back with his oar. 'Who are they?' Aeneas asked. 'They are those who came here straight from death,' said the Sybil sadly. 'Without proper funeral rites they may not cross, and are doomed for at least a hundred years to wait here, aimless and desolate.'

The Sybil then showed Charon the golden bough and unwillingly he took the living Aeneas and the Sybil across. They threw drugged honeycakes to Cerberus, the three-headed dog who guarded the entrance to the Kingdom of Hades. Cerberus fell asleep and they passed safely. In the Mourning Fields they saw the spirit of Dido, but though Aeneas called to her she did not speak nor even look at him.

Where the road divided, one fork leading to Elysium and the other to Tartarus, they heard the cries of those who had been guilty of grave sin and now endured everlasting punishment. Tantalus, reaching for food and drink that always slipped from his grasp, Ixion bound to his wheel, and Sisyphus for ever rolling his stone uphill. Aeneas, led by the Sybil, went on to Elysium, to the beautiful Fields of the Blest, and there they found his father.

Anchises stretched out his arms in welcome. 'Ah, dear son,' he said, 'you have come. Truly your love for me is strong, for it has brought you safely on this perilous journey.' Aeneas would have embraced him, but though he cried, 'Let me have your hand, dear Father,' and tried to enfold Anchises in his arms, his father's shade slipped from his clasp with no more substance than air.

Anchises now began to tell his son something of the proud empire which would come from the settlement he would found in Italy. And he showed him the ghosts of those who were not yet ready to go to the upper world. Pointing to a dimly lit corner where misty figures moved gently to and fro, he said, 'There are the souls of those who will drink from Lethe, the river of forgetfulness, before they are reborn on earth, remembering nothing that has happened before. Some are those who will create the Roman Empire; Romulus from whom the imperial city will take her name, and Julius Caesar, the conqueror, whose realm will reach to the ends of the earth.' Then Anchises tried to explain to Aeneas the divine mysteries of life and death, which now, having shed his mortality, he could understand. He showed his son many other strange sights; together they wandered freely amongst the spirits, and over hills and plains, and talked long before Anchises led Aeneas and the Sybil to the ivory gates which opened into the upper world. Before leaving, Aeneas placed the golden branch at the entrance of Queen Persephone's apartments in tribute to her.

When he returned from this astonishing journey, Aeneas went back to his companions. The ships set out once more and the voyagers sailed north, past the island of Circe the enchantress. Another day's journey north, and they reached the mouth of the river Tiber.

They landed and, as provisions had become short and they were very hungry, they quickly gathered wild berries to eat on rounds of bread. After they had eaten the berries and were chewing the flat cakes, Ascanius shouted out, laughing:

'Look! We are eating the plates.'

Thus the Harpies' strange prediction did come true! Following an ancient custom, Aeneas poured out libations: to the earth, to the nymphs and streams, to his goddess mother and to Zeus. Lightning flashed and there was thunder in a blue sky, showing that the gods had accepted the offering.

Latinus, king of Latium, as that country was called, had one daughter, Lavinia. Many princes wished to marry her, but it had been foretold that she was to marry a foreign prince. Aeneas sent heralds with a gold cup, along with the sceptre, diadem, and robe of King Priam to King Latinus, who then invited him to the palace. Hera was still unwilling to allow Aeneas success even at the end of his quest. She sent Alecto, one of the Furies, to start a quarrel between the Trojan voyagers and the Latins. Alecto took one of the snakes from her head and thrust it at night into the queen's bosom. Queen Amata, waking up in terror, as from a nightmare, screamed to her husband:

'This stranger Aeneas must not marry our daughter!'

'We cannot escape destiny,' said King Latinus. 'The Sybil

of Cumae has prophesied it, and it must be.'

In a frenzy, caused by the poison in her blood, the queen rushed out into the woods and, in her deluded state, joined with other women in the rites of the Dionysian mysteries. It was many days before she recovered her reason.

Hera sent Alecto next to Turnus, a wealthy prince in love with the princess Lavinia. She whispered to him:

'This foreigner, Aeneas, wants to take your bride away, so you must attack him.'

When Turnus refused, she took off her disguise, and maddened the prince with her snake locks and burning eyes, and the torch she threw at him. In her power at last, he set off with his army against Aeneas.

Hera now made Alecto cause more trouble by driving a tame stag, belonging to the royal herdsman, across Ascanius' path when he was out hunting. Ascanius shot the stag, and in the resulting quarrel some subjects of Latinus were killed, but the king still did nothing, saying only:

'I will not fight a war over this!'

So great Hera herself came down to earth. She went to the city and burst open the gates of Janus. These gates were closed in times of peace, and when they stood open, it meant beyond any doubt that the country was at war.

Aeneas had too few soldiers to fight all those who came against him. But the river god, wearing a long white robe, and with a garland of reeds on his head, appeared to him.

'Aeneas! Take heart, you will overcome your enemies. Tomorrow you will see a great white sow under an ilex tree, as proof that, after thirty years, Ascanius your son will build a new city as was prophesied. And, Aeneas, you must sacrifice to Hera, and pray that she cease her enmity towards you. King Evander, a Greek, will be your ally.'

Aeneas sailed on up the river Tiber and on the way saw the sow and her piglets. His mother, Aphrodite, brought him a suit of armour, richly ornamented with shining gold and brass, and a wonderful shield decorated with pictures of the future Rome. These had been made for him by the god Hephaestus, the armourer of Olympus. King Evander came at the head of his army to help Aeneas.

There was fierce war for many months. Then Zeus spoke to Hera, and persuaded her that she could not continue to struggle against Fate. But Hera, though at last willing that Aeneas fulfil his destiny, asked for one favour. Because she hated the name Trojan, it must be heard no more. The Latins and the Trojans should become one people, called Latins. Zeus agreed.

Hera ceased her persecution of Aeneas and it was by her intervention that he overcame Turnus. Thus the war ended, and the story of the Romans began.

When he was settled in the new land, Aeneas built shrines and altars to the gods where worship was conducted according to the old rites and custom. The ceremonies and the stories connected with the Immortals of Olympus were soon adopted by the Latins into their own beliefs, as the connection with Cumae increased and more Greeks came to Latium. But as time passed and new temples were built, and images and statues appeared in sacred precincts, there were changes to accommodate the needs of a developing nation, more practical and less poetic and imaginative than the people of Troy and Greece. And, three hundred years later, when Rome had become a city of consequence, the gods were completely Latinised under their Roman names. Great Zeus, the Father of gods and men was mighty Jove (or Jupiter) the Thunderer, and his consort was re-named Juno; Venus was the goddess of love and Eros, her son, had become the dimpled cherub, Cupid. The Greek god Ares, quarrelsome, and a stirrer-up of strife, but not aggressively warlike, had become Mars, the terrible Roman god of war—a fitting deity for a military and world-conquering people. Demeter was called Ceres and her daughter's name changed to Proserpina, while Dis or Pluto, ruler of the Kingdom of the Dead, was the name given to Hades. Dionysus, the Greek hero-god, shorn of his most important attributes, became Bacchus, the gross god of wine and revelry.

Aeneas did marry Lavinia. He founded the city of Lavinium, which he named in her honour, and he ruled it for three years. After his death, his spirit went, by the will of Zeus, to the Heavenly Plains, and he was succeeded by his son. Ascanius, calling himself Iulus, established Alba Longa as his capital, and in due course mighty Rome was built fifteen miles to the north-west, where it now stands.

So the prophecy for Aeneas, that he should found a 'new Troy', was in the end fulfilled.

The Founding of Rome

The descendants of Aeneas ruled for many generations in Alba Longa without strife until the time of Amulius. He seized the throne from the rightful king, his brother, Numitor, and drove Numitor away from the city to live in retirement on his private estate. To make sure that his brother's three children could not dispute the succession with his own heirs, Amulius had the boys ambushed and killed, and sent their sister Ilia, to the temple of Mars as a Vestal Virgin—which meant that she would never marry. But his wicked plans failed, for Ilia gave birth to twin boys, Romulus and Remus, and everyone believed that the god Mars was their father. Amulius imprisoned Ilia. Then he summoned two trusted servants and told them to steal the babies from the temple and drown them in the river.

Now the Tiber was then in full flood, and the men, not wanting to kill the infants, left them in their cradle on the river's bank, thinking the rising water would surely overturn the cradle and drown the twins. They told the king they had carried out his orders. But when the waters rushed over the bank the cradle floated and became a boat for Romulus and Remus. It was carried downstream and left in a sandy haven at the foot of the Palatine mountain. A she-wolf coming down to the river to drink heard the babies crying, and was led by a woodpecker to the cradle. Both these creatures were connected with Mars. The wolf fed the twins with her milk, licked them clean of the river mud, and carried them up to her mountain den. The woodpecker constantly flew around and brought berries and other offerings. In the temple

it was thought that the immortal god had spirited his children away.

Some weeks later Faustulus, a shepherd employed by Numitor, found the twins playing with the wolf's cubs at the mouth of the cave. The mother being absent he quickly picked them up and took them home to his childless wife.

So Romulus and Remus, princes of the royal house of Alba, were brought up as shepherd lads. They grew into strong, handsome young men and soon were able to attack the bandits who plundered travellers on the lonely mountain roads. They gave the spoils to their foster-parents and to other poor shepherd families. One day the robbers laid a trap for the youths. They caught Remus and took him before Numitor. The brigand chief, posing as an honest citizen, accused him of poaching on Numitor's land. Romulus went to his brother's help. The lordly bearing of the young men had already caused some comment among the ordinary people, and when Numitor saw them he was struck by their appearance and asked their parentage. Remus told how Faustulus had found them as babies, and Numitor realised they must be his grandsons. He embraced them and proudly showed them to the people. 'Look now on Romulus and Remus,' he cried, 'the rightful princes of the kingdom and my heirs.'

Romulus and Remus made a surprise attack on the usurping king: they killed Amulius, restored their grandfather to his throne and released their mother. Then they left Alba Longa to build a new city at the place where they had been rescued by the wolf. The fig tree which grew on the river bank, the wolf's cave and the shepherd's hut were preserved as sacred places, and the foundations of the new city were laid on the Palatine hill.

Then the time came when they had to decide which should be king. Romulus and Remus quarrelled as their grandfather and his brother had done. They asked the oracle for a sign, and the answer was favourable to Romulus. From that moment the twin brothers were no longer friends. Romulus worked out plans for streets and buildings and other details; Remus jeered at all he did. One day while watching men at work on the fortifications Remus jumped over the yet low wall. Instantly he was knocked down and killed, and his body thrown into the foundations of the battlements. For he had committed sacrilege; a city's walls, except for the gates, were holy and inviolable.

Thus Romulus was left to rule the new city, which he called Rome. He built temples to the gods of his Trojan forefathers and to the gods of the Latins, with majestic temples to Jupiter and Mars towering above them all. He laid down a code of civil law and founded an order of citizens, or 'fathers' to help administer the law and rule the city: and from this order of City Fathers later came the patricians of Rome. Romulus also established a sanctuary on the slopes of the Palatine hill for runaway slaves. And then, by a bold plan, he provided wives for the young men who had come with him from Alba Longa. A neighbouring people were the Sabines, and Romulus invited them to Rome, to watch sword play, wrestling and other sports. At the height of the festivities the young men of Rome suddenly seized the unmarried Sabine girls and took them for their wives. The angry parents were forced to return home without their daughters. Soon, however, the king of the Sabines, Titus Tatius, came at the head of an army to reclaim the captured girls.

Now it happened that the daughter of the commander of the outer defences was greedy for money and jewellery. She offered to show the Sabines a secret way in if her reward could be what each soldier wore on his left arm. Tarpeai meant their gold bracelets, but the soldiers as they passed her showed their opinion of her treachery by throwing at her the shields they carried on the left arm, and she was crushed to death beneath the weight. Romulus, still in command of the inner city, was able to show Titus that the Sabine women were honourably regarded as full citizens of Rome, not as slaves, and that they were happy with their husbands, for the captured women emerged in a body, refused to return home and called on their king not to fight. Thereupon peace was made and the two peoples lived in harmony.

In Olympus Mars took off his helmet and armour and stood before great Jupiter, his father, and he said, 'The time has come, noble sire, now that Rome's fortunes are secure and no longer depend upon one man alone, to keep the promise made to me when you said, "There will be a son of yours who will be raised to the blue vaults of the celestial heights." I pray you let me take Romulus from earth and bring him among the gods.'

Almighty Jupiter gave consent. He covered the world with dark clouds and created a terrifying thunderstorm. Accompanied by thunder and lightning Mars drove his chariot with all speed till his horses came to rest on the summit of the Palatine, where Romulus sat with his council, dispensing kindly justice to his people. Mars caught him up from the midst of the assembly and drove back to the home of the gods. The earthly body of Romulus dissolved into thin air. In its place he received godlike beauty and form, and was given the name of Quirinus. Some time later he appeared in a dream to a prominent elder of the city, and explained that he was now

Quirinus, a god of the Romans, and should be worshipped with Jupiter and Mars.

Thus was the prophecy fulfilled. More than four hundred years before, great Zeus, soothing the anxiety of Aphrodite for Aeneas, had promised a safe ending to her son's wanderings and glory for his descendants.

Rome, the city founded by Romulus of the line of Aeneas, later became the greatest city in Italy and then the greatest city in the world.

The Golden Ass

Lucius Apuleius, a wealthy young Greek from Africa, was
travelling through Greece on business. As he rode along the
way to Thessaly, he fell in with two other travellers and
their talk turned to mysteries, marvels and magic, then to the
power of a certain witch in the district. The subject fascinated
Lucius; he wanted to learn more about magic and witchcraft,
for to understand and be able to practise this strange, dark
art would give a man great power.

At last he reached the town of Hypata. A friend at home
had given him a letter of introduction to Milo, a rich merchant
of the town. Lucius found the house and knocked at the door,
and the slave girl who opened it took his letter to her master.
Lucius was invited to stay at Milo's house for as long as he
was in Hypata.

As he was very hot and dusty from the journey, he went
off to the public baths. On the way back he met some
friends, one of whom warned him:

'Milo's wife is a witch. You will have to be very careful.
She likes young men, but if you displease her she may put a
spell on you.'

'I'm not afraid,' said Lucius. He was, in fact, excited by the
news, and hurried back to Milo's house.

'This is my chance to learn more about witches and
spells,' he said to himself. 'But the first thing I must do is
to make friends with the slave girl, Fotis.'

As often as he could Lucius talked with Fotis, and soon
won her admiration and friendship. He told her how interested
he was in magic, and he begged her to let him watch her

mistress at work with her spells and witchcraft. So one evening, Fotis took him upstairs and, through a crack in the attic wall, he watched Milo's wife rub herself all over with ointment. Gradually, as she rubbed the ointment into her skin, her nose became a curved beak, her feet curled into talons with claws, feathers grew all over her, and her arms became wings. She was an owl. She flew out of the window and over the roofs to meet her latest lover.

Now that Lucius had seen the witch change herself into a bird he too wanted to fly over the roofs of the town.

'Please, Fotis,' he begged, 'steal some of your mistress's magic ointment, and give it to me.'

At first Fotis was unwilling to do this. She was afraid of her mistress, who had often beaten her, but at last she was won over. She went to the cabinet in the attic and stole a box of magic ointment for Lucius.

Eagerly he took the box from her hand and rubbed himself all over with the ointment. He felt himself changing, and flapped his arms like wings. But his arms did not become wings, something quite different happened to him. His ears grew long and hairy, and his hands bunched together and became hard without fingers. They were hoofs. He suddenly had a long tail. His head felt enormous and his nose and mouth were huge and hairy. He called out to Fotis but all he could say was 'Hee-Haw!' He was a donkey.

Fotis was horrified.

'I've brought the wrong ointment,' she wailed. 'Luckily I know the cure. It's very simple. Wait till morning and I'll take you into the garden. There you can eat roses, and as soon as you have eaten them you'll become a man again. But tonight you cannot sleep in your room in the house. Whatever would the slaves think in the morning if they found a donkey in your bed? No, that's impossible.'

So she led him downstairs, out of the house and into the stable. Lucius was not worried. The other donkey would make friends with him and his own white horse would surely be good company for one night.

But it did not happen that way. Lucius's white horse did not recognise his master. Why should he? And the other donkey was jealous of him. So the white horse and the donkey ganged up to keep him away from the food they wanted for themselves.

Lucius looked round the stable from the corner where he was sheltering from their hoofs and teeth. He saw a sight which could help him out of the pickle he was in. Roses! They were twined round a shrine put there in honour of Epona, the goddess with a mare's head.

He waited for his chance, moved quietly towards the pillar which supported the goddess and her shrine, and stretched up his head to the roses. Immediately his own slave, who was groom to his white horse, beat him for daring to try to eat the roses on the shrine. He was only a donkey and these were the roses dedicated to a goddess. Again and again, Lucius reached up to the roses. Again and again the slave beat him, till poor Lucius had to go back to his corner. He was consoled when he remembered that Fotis had promised

239

to bring him roses first thing in the morning. He had only to be patient and all would be well.

But it was not to be. During the night, thieves broke into Milo's house. Now, Milo possessed great wealth, and the thieves could not themselves carry off all the treasure they found. So they came down to the stable and loaded up the white horse and the two donkeys, one of whom of course was Lucius.

Lucius, being really a man, knew what was happening and called for help. But all he could shout was 'Hee-Haw!' and the thieves beat him for making a noise that might wake the neighbours.

On the way out of town they passed a garden with roses. Lucius knew that if he ran into the garden, ate the roses and became a young man again, the thieves would kill him; they would either think he was a wizard or be afraid he would betray them, since he had seen all that happened. So, poor Lucius had to plod on out of town, carrying a heavy load of stolen treasure, and miss this chance of changing back into a man.

At the first halt, a village where the thieves had friends, the white horse and the two asses were unloaded and turned into a paddock to rest and to graze. Lucius did not like grass, so he looked round for something better to eat. There was a vegetable garden quite near and he broke into that, for he was very hungry.

When the gardener saw him there eating his vegetables, he attacked him with a stick.

'Get out of there!' he shouted, and hit Lucius. Lucius kicked him. Then the gardener's wife came running, calling to the dogs:

'Bite him! Bite the brute! Tear him to pieces!'

Again Lucius was beaten, and chased by savage dogs as well. He began to understand what it was like to live the life of a donkey.

Next day he decided to lie down and refuse to go another step carrying such a heavy load. Luckily for him the other donkey did this first. The thieves were not going to be bothered with a lazy donkey and they just threw the stubborn animal over a cliff. Lucius decided it was better to remain alive and be beaten than to be killed, so he went on quietly with his burden. After some time they came to the thieves' cave. Here Lucius and the white horse were unloaded.

This cave was in charge of an old woman. The two animals were given plenty of barley, but it was uncooked, so Lucius left it all to the white horse and made his own meal from the loaves of bread the thieves had stored in the corner of the cave. He was eating his third basketful of bread when daylight came.

Now, during the night, the thieves had gone off on another raid and at dawn they returned with their loot, and brought with them a beautiful girl called Charite. They had carried her off just before her wedding, and they intended to keep her prisoner till her father paid a large ransom for her.

Lucius had to work day after day and carry heavy loads for the robbers. He was continually beaten, and so cruelly used that he became lame and this caused his masters to treat him more brutally than ever.

One day when the robber band was absent, he determined in desperation to run away. He struggled until he broke the rope that held him. The old woman clung to the broken rope, but the maiden, Charite, seized it from her, and quickly jumped on his back, so that they escaped together.

'I'll look after you, little ass, if you take me safely home,' said the girl.

Of course she thought of him as a donkey, and when at the crossroads Lucius turned to what he knew was the safest way, she insisted on going along the road which would lead most directly to her father's house. And on this road they met the robbers coming back. So poor Lucius was caught and beaten again, and Charite was chained to a post in the cave.

While the thieves were discussing what to do with the girl, the thief who had been left behind to watch Milo's house returned to the gang.

'All the people of Hypata are blaming Lucius Apuleius for robbing Milo's house. They don't know where he is. He disappeared at the time of the robbery, and hasn't been seen since.'

'No, no!' shouted Lucius but as he sounded just like a donkey no one took any notice.

'On my way back,' continued the spy, 'I met a tall young beggar. He agreed to join us and is waiting down the road.'

The beggar was brought in.

'I'm not really a beggar,' he explained. 'I was once a bandit captain. Since then I have become a master thief. I'll share my spoil with you.'

He cut open his rags and out tumbled two thousand gold pieces. He was so tall and strong, and so clearly very successful, that when he offered to be their new captain, the band of thieves accepted him.

Actually he was Charite's sweetheart. He had been looking for her everywhere, and now he had found her. As they trusted him, he was able to make the robbers drunk and tie them up. Then he put Charite on the donkey's back and took her home. When she was safe, he returned with his friends to the cave. There they threw some of the thieves over a cliff, the others they beheaded. The loot from the robbers' cave they gathered together and took home for the public treasury. Charite and her sweetheart were married and Lucius was given a feast of meal and hay. He would rather have had the meat the dogs were eating in the kitchen. But of course nobody knew he was a very unusual animal.

To Charite and her husband Lucius was only a donkey, so sending him off to live happily on a farm was what they thought best for him. They were not to know that the farm-bailiff's wife would harness him to the mill and make him walk round and round for a very long day, and beat him again and again. Even in the pasture he was the unluckiest donkey alive, being kicked and bitten by the other animals.

One day word came that Charite and her husband had died. The slaves packed up all the valuables in the house and set off for the next town beyond the mountains. Here Lucius was sold to an old priest called Philebus.

His work was to carry on his back a statue of the goddess Cybele for travelling priests who, wearing gaudy robes, made a great noise on horns, cymbals and tambourines, and danced and sang to attract attention so that people would give them money. Now these priests were really a band of rascals, making a show of piety, and deceiving poor, ignorant folk who were afraid of offending the goddess if they did not give presents to her priests. The band travelled mostly through the country, avoiding big towns.

One day a religious farmer, who believed they were holy men, invited them into his house for supper, and to spend the night. Lucius was tethered in the farmyard. But a dog stole a joint of venison from the kitchen. This was to be the principal dish, and there was no other meat. The cook's wife had the cruel idea of cutting a great chunk from the donkey. She dragged Lucius into the kitchen and told her husband it would be easy to prepare a roast of donkey so that it tasted like venison. Lucius, who could of course understand all she said, was terrified. He broke his halter, escaped from the cook-house and dashed into the dining room where the farmer was seated with his guests. Now as a slave had just come to tell them that a mad dog was loose and had attacked both men and animals, everyone at once thought that the donkey had been bitten by the mad dog. They were all too frightened to try to catch him, and instead hurried off to find weapons with which to subdue him. Lucius then ran from the dining room and took refuge in the chief priest's bedroom. Thankfully the terrified men locked the door, and shut him away. So Lucius was able to have a peaceful night's sleep in a comfortable bed.

In the early morning he heard whispers outside the door. 'That ass is surely dead,' said one. 'I agree,' said another, 'the poison and madness will have killed him.' They unlocked the door and opened it a chink and saw the donkey alive, and standing sober and quiet in the middle of the room. Then

243

one man came with a basin of water and put it down on the floor. He explained to his companions, 'The ass seems quiet enough, but we shall see. If he drinks, then he is well and has all his ass's wits. If he turns from the water trembling with fear, that will be proof of his madness.'

Lucius heard this with some relief. He thrust his head into the basin, and drank in great gulps as though he had a mighty thirst. The men were no longer afraid. They took him down, placed the statue on his back and set out with their fellows for the next village. Here they stayed for some days as guests of the inhabitants, who fed and cared for them. The rascally priests went round begging from house to house, and also made a great deal of money by telling fortunes to the simple, credulous people. Then one night, Lucius knew not why, they quickly packed up and went off secretly in the dark by a side lane. Soon, however, they were overtaken by a band of angry villagers, carrying lanterns and fully armed. They seized the priests and bound them, crying, 'Where is the gold cup you have stolen? Don't think you can rob us under cover of religion and then escape cunningly at night.' The priests laughed and joked and protested they had not stolen a gold cup, and asked the villagers to search them. This was done, and nothing was found. Then a man came to Lucius and searched his trappings and found the cup hidden in folds of the statue's garments. The priests were taken back and put in prison. The villagers purified the cup and the statue and placed them in their own temple.

Next day Lucius was put up for sale in the market. A baker bought him, and used him cruelly. All day and every day the donkey had to grind corn. If he stopped or slowed his pace he was beaten; the food was poor, and hardly enough to keep him alive. In the stable there were many old miserable horses: lame, covered with sores, half blind, and all showing their bones. Poor Lucius wondered if he would be released from this master before he too came to the same wretched state.

Happily for him the baker died, and Lucius was sold to a

gardener. He was a poor hard-working man, who every day used to load the donkey with produce for the nearby market, then ride him home. This master was kind to Lucius and shared his simple food with him, but as he was very poor and without even a proper house, it was also a poor life for Lucius.

One day as Lucius slowly plodded homewards, his master on his back, they passed a military camp and were accosted in the roadway by a Roman soldier. '*Quorsum vacuum ducis asinum?*' he said. The gardener, not understanding Latin, rode on. Then the soldier struck him on the back and demanded the ass to carry his arms and equipment. When Lucius's master protested, the soldier tried to drag the donkey away. Then there was a fight in which the gardener came off best. He seized the soldier's short sword and rode quickly to the refuge of a friend's house. Here the gardener was hidden in a deep chest and Lucius shut up in the attic. The centurion's friends accused the gardener of theft and the magistrate, learning where he had fled, searched the house. Lucius was so interested in the stir and tumult below that he looked out of the attic window. The shadow of his long ears on the opposite wall gave him away just when the officers had decided their search was fruitless. So the centurion made Lucius carry his arms and equipment to the garrison in a nearby town. Here he sold Lucius (though he had not paid a penny piece for him) to two brothers, a confectioner and cook, slaves of a nobleman, called Thyasus.

Now, after dinner, the two brothers always brought the left-overs to their room to have a feast, but before eating they would go off to the baths. Lucius took advantage of this and tasted a little from each dish. As time passed he grew greedy and ate more. The brothers began to blame each other for the missing food. They did not imagine that their donkey was taking it, for they had no idea he would like it. But when they noticed that the donkey was getting fat without eating any hay they began to suspect that something strange was happening.

One evening they pretended to go out as usual, but instead

watched through a peep-hole and saw the donkey eating from their supper dishes. They laughed and laughed, it was so funny. Lord Thyasus, hearing them, came to look, and he laughed too. Lucius was surprised when they all came into the room and gave him wine. Naturally he drank it, and just as a man would. The sight increased Lord Thyasus' amusement. He at once put this clever donkey into the care of a slave who was to teach him tricks—how to recline at table, how to lean on his elbow, how to wrestle and dance on two legs, and how to use sign language. Of course, being really a man, Lucius could have done all this without being taught.

Thyasus was appointed Lord Chief Justice of Corinth for five years. To make himself popular, he promised a three-day show with gladiators and wild animals, and acting, music and dancing. Thyasus began to use the donkey as his favourite mount and Lucius became a "golden ass" indeed, with gold trappings on his harness, red leather saddle, purple cloth, silver bit and silver bridle decorated with bells. Often, for the amusement of his friends, Thyasus would bring Lucius in to have dinner with them.

Such was the fame of Thyasus' donkey that in Corinth the crowds came out to see the golden ass and the Chief Justice in that order. The ass's keeper began to charge a fee to those who wanted to watch his tricks.

Now the winter was over: Spring had come, early flowers were in bloom, the time of roses was drawing near. Lucius was beginning to hope . . .

Then it was arranged that the donkey was to take a horrible part in the celebrations. He was to appear in a cage with a wicked woman and the wild beast which would devour her. Lucius was horrified. He was terribly frightened too. The wild animal might eat him instead, for how could it know that the woman only was the victim? On the first day of the festival, and just before the time for the donkey's appearance, Lucius suddenly realised that he was alone and unwatched, for all the men were busy getting the cage in position. 'Ye gods in heaven!' he said to himself. 'Now is my chance to escape.' He stole out of a side gate, and then galloped on and on till he was far from Corinth. Still he ran until he came to a busy port on the Saronic Sea. Avoiding the crowded streets, for he did not want to be seen, Lucius made his way to the shore. There, in a sandy hollow by the edge of the water, exhausted, he fell asleep. He awoke just as the full moon was rising from the sea. Lucius knew the moon was a goddess. So he ran to the water's edge and plunged his head seven times into the sea.

Piteously he prayed to the goddess of the moon, imploring her to have compassion on him and turn him again into a man. 'After all I have endured,' he cried, and great tears rolled down his hairy cheeks, 'I would rather die than continue to live as an ass.' Then he went back to his hollow and fell fast asleep again.

He awoke a second time to see a tall beautiful woman standing beside him. Long hair fell to her shoulders and framed her divine countenance. Upon her hair she wore a head-dress of precious stones and flowers. In the centre of her forehead was a round gleaming jewel resembling the moon. In one hand she held two coiled serpents, in the other stalks and ears of corn. Her flowing raiment shimmered in different colours when she moved: sometimes yellow, sometimes rose, sometimes like a flame of fire, and again sometimes dark and shadowed. The hem of her robe was edged with flowers. Over all a black cloak hung from her shoulders. On this glittering gold stars were cunningly set in the folds, and in the centre, shining like a cold flame, was a silver moon. A delicate, divine fragrance surrounded this heavenly being, who stooped over the poor donkey, and said, 'Behold, Lucius, I am come. Thy prayers and weeping have moved me to help thee. I am she that is Mother of all things, chief of powers divine, Queen of heaven. My divinity is adored throughout the world in different rites and by different names. Some think me Aphrodite, others Persephone or Hera, but the Ethiopians of the Orient, the Egyptians and the people of this country call me Queen Isis. So put away all sorrow, and listen to my command, for I will bring thee comfort.'

247

Then the goddess told him that the next day was a festival in her honour, and there would be a procession to the sea-shore.

'The High Priest will carry a garland of roses in his right hand,' said the goddess. 'You, Lucius, must join the procession quietly and eat the roses. When you have done this you will become a man again. In return, you must dedicate yourself to my service for the rest of your life.' And, after promising him that he would always have her divine protection if he proved himself worthy, the goddess vanished.

The poor ass, Lucius, trembling and sweating in a mixture of hope and fear, yet exalted by the heavenly vision, bathed himself in the sea. Then, as day began to dawn, he left the shore and went towards the town. Soon after, the sun rose dispelling the early morning sea mists. The streets were crowded with excited people, for this was a day of joyful celebration. Many men and women carried garlands and other offerings. Some were dressed as characters from legends, or as animals and buffoons. A long procession, led by singers and dancers, came towards the sea-shore, pushing their way through the watching crowds. Then there was the sound of rhythmic chanting. Officials cleared a path for the holy procession from the temple. Those who walked in front threw flowers and sweet balm on the ground, and bystanders strewed blossoms and herbs and fragrant essences in the pathway of the priests. First came young men dressed in white, singing a hymn to the goddess, and following them priests in their robes, carrying sacred relics, images and symbols of the temple rites. A beautiful cow, her hoofs polished and her hide gleaming like silk, led by solemn attendants, represented the goddess, and, following her, came yet more priests. One bore in his arms the model of a sailing ship, made of citron wood; there was a gold roof to the cabin, and inscriptions on the white linen sails and on the prow. Then came the great High Priest. In his right hand he carried a garland of roses!

Lucius, trembling with hope, watched him and had no eyes for the great number who still came after. The High Priest was now near. Lucius edged his way softly through the press of people, and came up behind him. As the goddess had promised the priest turned and stopped and held out the roses to the ass. Lucius chewed quickly. At once his transformation took place. The rough hair fell off, his head became small, the large ears shrank, his hands and feet came back to him, the tail vanished: he was a man again. The priest ordered a servant to give Lucius his outer robe, and then he smiled and said, 'O, my friend Lucius, after enduring such hardship and misfortune as the result of thy misguided curiosity about witchcraft, thou art now safe, and delivered from thy misery by the mercy of the goddess Isis. Therefore rejoice and by thy future deeds show thy gratitude.' The news that a donkey had become a man quickly spread among the people. Everyone crowded round in amazement to look at Lucius.

But he quietly joined in the procession and ignored the curiosity of the people. The procession went on along the shore until it reached the very spot where as a donkey he had spent the night. The priest purified the model ship, then blessed it, put it down in the water, and prayed that Isis would protect all merchant shipping during the coming months. The little vessel was filled to overflowing with large and small gifts, then it was pushed away from the shore. The sails filled and it sped over the water and out to the open sea. All watched till the ship was out of sight, and then broke into a hymn of praise because the goddess had accepted the first fruits of the season's navigation. When the ship could be seen no longer the priest's procession, in the same order, returned to the temple, the people following.

All the images and holy relics were restored to their places. The High Priest said a prayer, gave a blessing from the goddess and dismissed the people to their homes.

Lucius stayed on alone, and remained long, kneeling before the silver statue of Isis, (the great mother goddess who had released him from his bondage) remembering all the misery he had endured while he had been the Golden Ass.

Other Retellings

GEORGE BAKER. *The Realms of Gold*. Illustrated by Geoffrey Fraser. U.L.P. 1954. A connected narrative in thirty-two chapters, which summarises the first building of Troy, the *Iliad*, the *Odyssey*, the *Aeneid*, the hero tales and some minor myths, ending with a forecast of the might of Rome. The connecting link is the house and line of Pelops and their sufferings under the curse of Myrtilus, which is expiated only when Orestes, the last of the line, becomes ruler of Mycenae.

This is a brilliant crystallisation of a vast field of legend. I do not recommend it for younger children, just because there is so much in it that it is almost breathless, leaping from name to name and story to story. But for older children, who already know some Greek legends or have read several books about them, and for young adults who want to find out how some tale is related to others, it is interesting reading, important in that it presents one detailed aspect of a 'whole' view and useful for reference. The style is mostly straightforward narrative. As well as end-paper maps there is an excellent index of characters, so that all tales included within the main plan can be easily found. The gods are referred to only as and when they appear in connection with the lives of humans. Nothing is said of the glory of Olympus or of worship in earth's temples.

The production is pleasant (not as youthful in appearance as the books by Roger Lancelyn Green) and since many of the illustrations are either decorations or stylised pictures, the book would be at home on almost any bookshelf.

The names are given in their Greek forms.

ALFRED J. CHURCH. *The Iliad and the Odyssey of Homer*. Afterword by Clifton Fadiman. Illustrated by Eugene Karlin. Macmillan New York, 1964.

This handsomely produced volume from the U.S.A., with strangely gentle, stylised full page drawings (mainly portraits, with details of drapery, armour, instruments and utensils carefully depicted) is a new edition of the version Church wrote for children early in the century (1905–7). For those who know his *Story of the Iliad* and *Story of the Odyssey* the title is, therefore, rather misleading (although copyright dates give a clue), and the double Table of Contents, the combined list of illustrations and the continuous page numbering obscure the fact that these are two separate books, so it is surprising that the *Odyssey* should begin 'A great many years ago there was a very famous siege of a city called Troy'.

The texts are simpler, non-archaic rewritings of the earlier books, so this is an edition which has much to give to children not to be found in other retellings. But occasional archaisms in sentences otherwise modern are awkward and some similes, being reworded and cut, are changed in meaning and do not sound like Church.

As all of Church is out of print in Britain we can only be grateful that the Americans keep his memory green in such a handsome work. American spelling and Greek names are used except where Church himself used the Latin forms, in 'Ulysses' and 'Bacchus'.

Obtainable in Britain from Collier Macmillan.

PADRAIC COLUM. *The Children's Homer* (1918); *The Golden Fleece* (1921). Illustrated by Willy Pogany. Reprinted 1966. Macmillan New York.

Reprints of books which enjoyed esteem and popularity forty odd years ago. Today the uncrowded page, with clear type and many large and small drawings, is pleasant to the eye, and children of from eight to ten, even with many more books to choose from, will find Colum a graphic storyteller.

The Children's Homer begins and ends with the adventures of

Odysseus, and the whole story of the Trojan war is told to Telemachus by Menelaus and Helen in Sparta. By this re-assembling the *Iliad* is contained within the *Odyssey*.

In *The Golden Fleece* Colum used a somewhat similar device; the Argonauts hear a number of stories told aloud by Orpheus and others while on their voyages to and from Colchis. The last section of the book contains accounts of Meleager, Peleus and Thetis, Theseus, Heracles, Admetus and Alcestis, and Orpheus and Eurydice. Unfortunately, as both Table of Contents and Index are lacking, there is no guide in either book to individual tales.

Colum, writing in flowing, poetic prose, is never sentimental, but his deliberately archaic style is uneven and sometimes awkwardly forced. In spite of this, and of much invention and rearrangement, he has kept the flavour of ancient Greece. Names are given in their modified Greek form, but American spelling, of course. (English orders to Collier Macmillan in London.)

LEON GARFIELD and EDWARD BLISHEN. *The God Beneath the Sea.* Illustrated by Charles Keeping. Longmans, 1970. Awarded the Library Association's 1970 Carnegie Medal.

> 'As children . . . from these great stories we had drawn some of our earliest and most powerful impressions of the nature of human destiny, and of the quality and force of human passion . . . we felt there was room for an attempt to tell the mythological story . . . as a continuous narrative . . . a total tale that, while it would miss out much in terms of the quantity that is offered, would miss out as little as possible in terms of the entire meaning of the whole mythological structure . . . To provide such a telling (of the myths) as will, for young readers of our time, make them of that order of sources of understanding of life that they were to us, long ago.' From the authors' Afterword.

A selection of Greek myths, based on ancient sources, beginning with the fall of the infant Hephaestus (the god of the title) into the sea, when he was thrown from Olympus by Hera, and ending with a second fall when Zeus in anger cast the 'vile, twisted thing' down to earth. Between these first and last chapters the stories of earth's creation and of the Titans, giants and Olympian gods, up to the birth of Ares, are told to young Hephaestus during his years with Thetis and Eurynome. The making of men by Prometheus, his theft of fire and his punishment; the story of Pandora; Zeus' visit to Lycaon; the Flood; Demeter and Core (the longest single story); Hermes and Chione; and Sisyphus and Autolycus, are the chief subjects of the rest of the book.

Apart from accepting both expulsions of Hephaestus from Olympus the authors' other variants are: the death of both Uranus and Cronus (pursued by the Furies and insane) and Pan as co-existent with the first Titans.

In this vividly imaginative reconstruction the gods, immense in physical stature, indulge in the whole range of human emotion, but rarely show majestic fortitude in pain or anger. The prose, rich in verbal sounds, matches in intensity, violence and emphasis on love and passion this aspect of Greek mythology. Keeping's fourteen large and powerful drawings are likewise his own interpretations rather than exact illustrations of the text, four being used twice. A handsomely lavish production.

ROGER LANCELYN GREEN. *Heroes of Greece and Troy*. Illustrated by Helen Copley and C. Chamberlain. Bodley Head, 1960.

"The tale of the Greek Heroes, the history of the Heroic age, as the single whole the Greeks believed it to be . . . told from the ancient authors." In thirty-five chapters Roger Lancelyn Green has included a tremendous amount of material. He begins with the Coming of the Immortals (an introductory and explanatory chapter) and covers the hero sagas, the *Iliad* and the *Odyssey;* and works into the main narrative many shorter myths. The account of the Flood, from Ovid, is the destruction of the world by Zeus because of the wickedness of the neighbours of Baucis and Philemon, who with Deucalion and Pyrrha are saved. In spite of the very wide scope of the book many details not usually given in retellings of the *Iliad* and the hero tales are included, with a good deal of imaginary conversation and description.

This is an honest retelling, suitable for children from any age at which they can read fluently, and important in that it shows the interrelation of many stories in one continuous tale. R. L. Green knows his subject thoroughly; he also knows Greece. Each chapter is introduced by an appropriate verse and a decorative drawing. The type though small is clear, and the general appearance attractive to children. It is a pity that there is no index since the chapter headings cannot cover all the individual stories included in the text.

Greek names are used throughout. There is a list of the gods, with their equivalent Latin names, and two clear maps.

Originally Puffin, 1958—*Tales of Greek Heroes*
—*The Tale of Troy*

ROGER LANCELYN GREEN. *Old Greek Fairy Tales*. Illustrated by Ernest H. Shepard. G. Bell & Sons. 1958.

An attractive-looking book of sixteen stories from Greek myth and legend—some famous, others, as for example, 'Rhodope, or the Rosy Slipper' and 'The Three Wishes', less familiar—written, for the most part, in the formal timeless style associated with traditional folklore. No difficult names are used, the gods are represented by a king, queen or prince with magical powers, and the 'once upon a time' tales have such titles as 'The Prince and the Flying Horse' (Bellerophon), 'The Boy who talked with the Beasts' (Melampus), 'The Invisible Prince' (Eros and Psyche), 'A Crafty King' (Sisyphus).

Young children of seven, eight and nine, who read them now as fairy tales, will recognise them when they meet them again later in their literary context of heroic legend and family chronicle.

In the Preface and Author's Note Roger Lancelyn Green discusses his method of retelling, and gives his authorities and sources.

ROGER LANCELYN GREEN. *Tales the Muses Told*. Illustrated by Shirley Hughes. Bodley Head, 1965.

Except for the last four stories (under the heading 'Great Lovers and True Friends') this is a collection of nature myths: four stories under each group—'Flowers', 'Trees', 'Birds and Beasts' and 'Stars'. There are familiar tales, for example, Pegasus, Daphne, and Hyacinthus, as well as several not easily found elsewhere. The retelling is suitable for the 'romantic fairy-tale age' rather than for little children. The material is useful, also, to storytellers.

CHARLES KINGSLEY. *The Heroes*. Illustrated by H. M. Brock. Macmillan, 1856. New edition, illustrated by J. Kiddell Monroe. Dent, 1965.

These two editions are particularly attractive; there are many others. The heroes are Perseus, Jason and the Argonauts, and Theseus, and the stories are told in their most complete form. It is interesting to compare the Greek tales of Kingsley with those of Andrew Lang, who also includes the Argonauts and the adventures of Theseus and Perseus. Both were scholars and had positions of authority in the academic and literary world. Both wrote in these instances for children (Kingsley for his own family: Lang for his huge public family—the readers of his Fairy Tale books) and not as authorities but as storytellers to the young. Both freely adapted but Lang rather more than Kingsley—who on the whole simply leaves out what he does not want to include.

Kingsley, keeping closely to the spirit of the original sources, wrote in what is described as 'heroic style', and it is now old-fashioned. But the grandeur remains, and this is a fine retelling to read aloud to children, for there is mystery and majesty to all the tales, although each begins, 'Once upon a time'.

ANDREW LANG. *Tales of Troy and Greece*. Illustrated by Edward Bawden. Faber & Faber, 1962.

[*The Adventures of Ulysses*. Illustrated by J. Kiddell Monroe. Illustrated Children's Classics, Dent 1962.]

Originally published by Longmans in 1907, these reprints are most welcome because Lang's retelling, requiring no more effort to read than the later Fairy Books and the collections of romantic legends, is probably one of the *first* best books to give to children. The full account of Ulysses, from birth to death, occupies more than half the 284 pages of *Tales of Troy and Greece* and the whole of the Dent publication. The other stories are: 'The Fleece of Gold' (first published in 1903 in the U.S.A. as 'The Story of the Golden Fleece'), 'Theseus' and 'Perseus'. Lang writes in his own words as a storyteller but in a style conditioned by his thorough knowledge of the original sources. He ·rearranges and invents more than Kingsley and is more romantic and less heroic in his attitude. For example he describes the actual marriage of Theseus and Ariadne in Crete, and tells how she died on the voyage to Athens "with her hands in the hands of Theseus and his lips on her lips". There are few references to the gods and their part in the affairs of men. Helen is not promised to Paris by Aphrodite. She elopes with him because of their infatuation for each other.

There are minor inconsistencies (for Lang was often careless) but children are unlikely to notice them in reading these stories specifically written for their enjoyment.

Both editions are attractive and child-like. That published by Faber has clear type and unsentimental, 'martial' illustrations and is suitable in appearance for a wide age range.

Although the Latin 'Ulysses' is used all other names are in the Greek form.

SIR COMPTON MACKENZIE. *The Strongest Man on Earth*. Illustrated by T. Ritchie. Chatto, 1968.

Compton MacKenzie told Greek hero tales to young

children on a B.B.C. Television programme, the success of which prompted the publication of this book.

The production (small type, rather casual and sometimes sophisticated illustrations) will, unfortunately, not be so attractive to young readers as some other less good versions. The telling is a direct narration, in conversational style, without the usual padding of invented description and conversation—of the birth and youth of Heracles, all the Labours, and his death and translation to Olympus and immortality among the gods.

The author occasionally brings in other stories to do with a place or an event, and as 'himself' explains a geographical or historical reference, makes a contemporary comparison or puts in an aside, such as, 'that was what was called "a Sop to Cerberus" '. The six-page Prologue describes the world of Heracles, gives an account of the gods (and their Roman equivalents) and examples of words and expressions currently in use, connected with them and their attributes.

The whole little book is original, and, revealing MacKenzie's life-long love of Greek legends and of Greece, provides more than is suggested by its appearance and title.

KENNETH MACLEISH. *The Story of Aeneas*. Illustrated by Charles Keeping. Longman (Heritage of History Series) 1968.
'*The Story of Aeneas* is not in any sense a literal translation. It is an abridged and simplified version of the original story . . . an introduction to the *Aeneid* for those making their first acquaintance with Latin epic.' From the Author's note.

A dignified, fast-moving retelling in short sentences and with easy natural dialogue. It follows Virgil except that a final paragraph is added to give the marriage of Aeneas and Lavinia and the prediction of the founding of Rome.

Handled with authority and skilfully told, this is a useful book for storytellers, teachers and librarians to keep in mind, as well as a version for some children (from nine or ten upwards) and young people to read.

Interestingly some of Keeping's small illustrations, in particular those of the Souls of the Dead and the Death of

Rhoetes, forecast his dramatic drawings for *The God Beneath the Sea*.

Given a more spacious production (and without all those paragraph headings) this book could have been popular with children of a wide range in age, young adult readers and many for whom this series does not cater.

BARBARA LEONIE PICARD. *The Iliad of Homer; The Odyssey of Homer*. Illustrated by J. Kiddell Monroe. O.U.P. 1952.

These are very pleasant-looking books and come in age of reading before any of the retellings of Homer (except for Kingsley and Lang) listed here. The *Odyssey* is well done, a straightforward account which retains both the drama of the incidents and the sense of time in the hero's long voyage. The *Iliad* is reliable but for me lacks a certain power and grandeur.

JAMES REEVES. *Heroes and Monsters*. Illustrated by Sarah Nechamkin. Blackie, 1969.

Twenty plainly told, more or less unconnected stories including accounts of: Jason; Heracles; Perseus; Theseus; Odysseus; Eros and Psyche; and a number of well-known and lesser-known myths. It is perhaps unfortunate that the description of the gods appears in the introduction (which is followed by a Pronunciation Guide, with no page or story references) and so may not be read by children. Mr. Reeves takes his own stand on debatable points; Prometheus creates man on a general order from the gods and almost immediately steals fire from heaven; Zeus orders the creation of Pandora as man's companion and helpmate, and one of her gifts (from Athene) is *wisdom*. Apollo is said to be the father of both Phaethon and Orpheus. The type is clear and well-spaced and the page inviting to the eye of quick young readers.

N. B. TAYLOR. *The Aeneid of Virgil*. Illustrated by J. Kiddell Monroe. O.U.P., 1961.

259

Good clear type, many black and white illustrations for a full-length straightforward retelling. The beginning is re-arranged to allow the book to start with the Sack of Troy and Aeneas' preparation for his long voyage in search of a new home: it ends exactly where the *Aeneid* does, with the death of Turnus. A pity!—for children want to know what happened after. There is an alphabetical list of persons and places which occur in the story with a description but no page references, as for example, 'Evander: King of Arcadia; Venus: daughter of Jove; goddess of love and beauty; mother of Aeneas; Sicily: large island separated from Italy by the Straits of Messina.' The introduction gives an account of the Roman gods (and the author's own estimation of their characters) and also a short account of the causes of the Trojan war.

REX WARNER. *The Stories of the Greeks*. Illustrated with photographs. MacGibbon and Kee, 1967.

A handsome American production, in the original texts, of three books (published in England by MacGibbon and Kee in the 1950's): *Men and Gods* (1950)—retellings from Ovid's *Metamorphoses* and other Latin authors, and a translation from Apuleius of Eros and Psyche. The names of gods in their Latin form; *Greeks and Trojans* (1951)—a splendidly direct, dramatic account of the Trojan war, mainly from Homer's *Iliad*. Greek names for the gods in this and the third book; *The Vengeance of the Gods* (1954)—nine stories from Greek plays, the *Alcestis, Hippolytus* and five others of Euripides, the *Prometheus Bound* and *Agamemnon* of Aeschylus.

The retellings, straightforward narrative (with sometimes considerable imaginative dialogue and descriptions), is very readable, suitable for the teenage young as well as for the general reader looking for a comprehensive but uncomplicated version of the stories. Rex Warner concludes his explanatory Introduction to this three-in-one volume, with 'There is no pretension of scholarship. The aim has been simply "all for your delight".' Nevertheless, although the style is uneven, particularly in *Men and Gods*, Warner's wide knowledge of classical literature and history, while unobtrusive, clearly adds to the value of an important addition to contemporary versions of Greek Myths. In view of the book's spacious setting and lavish appearance it is difficult to understand the lack of a 'List of Illustrations' (sculpture and carvings, many ancient and mutilated), and any means of identification. And, with only a general Table of Contents, not individual guides to each part, a general Index to the whole would seem almost essential.

Index of Names and Subjects

Zeus, father of the gods, 29, 30, 36–40, 230; aegis of, 37, 180; and Aeneas, 222, 223, 224, 230; and Apple of Discord, 143–5, 146; and Baucis and Philemon, 122–8; and Semele, 81–2; and Thetis, 131–5, 142–4; and Trojan War, 165–6, 175–6, 178, 180, 183, 184, 187–8, 191, 192, 198, 200